America in the 21st Century: Political and Economic Issues

Role of Tax Preferences in Financial Infrastructure

America in the 21st Century: Political and Economic Issues

Additional books in this series can be found on Nova's website at:

https://www.novapublishers.com/catalog/index.php?cPath=23_29&seriesp=America+in+the+21st+Century%3A+Political+and+Economic+Issues

Additional E-books in this series can be found on Nova's website at:

https://www.novapublishers.com/catalog/index.php?cPath=23_29&seriespe=America+in+the+21st+Century%3A+Political+and+Economic+Issues

AMERICA IN THE 21ST CENTURY: POLITICAL AND ECONOMIC ISSUES

ROLE OF TAX PREFERENCES IN FINANCIAL INFRASTRUCTURE

MICHAEL D. SCOTT
EDITOR

Nova Science Publishers, Inc.
New York

For permission to use material from this book please contact us:
Telephone 631-231-7269; Fax 631-231-8175
Web Site: http://www.novapublishers.com

LIBRARY OF CONGRESS CATALOGING-IN-PUBLICATION DATA

Role of tax preferences in financial infrastructure / editor, Michael D. Scott.
p. cm.
Includes index.
ISBN 978-1-61668-546-1 (hardcover)
1. Tax expenditures--United States. 2. Tax incentives--United States. I. Scott, Michael D., 1965-
HJ4653.T22R65 2010
336.2'06--dc22

2010012280

Published by Nova Science Publishers, Inc. ✝ New York

CONTENTS

PREFACE

The federal government supports infrastructure investment in a variety of ways. However, the most common means of providing a tax subsidy for infrastructure investment, by offering a tax exemption for interest on state and local bonds, is generally viewed to be an inefficient way to subsidize state and local borrowing, largely because the revenue cost to the federal government may exceed the interest-cost subsidy provided to state and local governments by a substantial amount. This book assesses the role of tax preferences in infrastructure investments in the United States and discusses the types of tax preferences for state and local bonds, and it also considers how the current system of tax preference might change as a result of greater use of tax-credit bonds.

Chapter 1 - The Subcommittee on Select Revenue Measures of the House Committee on Ways and Means has scheduled a public hearing for March 16, 2006, on State and local government bonds. This document,[1] prepared by the staff of the Joint Committee on Taxation, provides a description of the present law and background relating to State and local government bonds.

Chapter 2 - The Committee on Ways and Means has scheduled a public hearing on October 29, 2008 on economic recovery, job creation and investment in America. Among the issues the Committee will consider is the ability of State and local governments to finance infrastructure needs. This document[1] provides a description of present law relating to tax-exempt bonds issued by State and local governments and a description of present law relating to tax-credit bonds, both of which operate to deliver a Federal subsidy to eligible borrowers, albeit by different mechanisms and with different degrees of efficiency. The document also provides background data and an economic discussion of tax-exempt bonds and tax-credit bonds.

Chapter 3 - The public and private sectors in the United States together spend over $500 billion a year on infrastructure projects, including highways and airports, water and energy utilities, dams, waste-disposal sites and other environmental facilities, schools, and hospitals. The federal government makes a significant contribution to that investment through its direct expenditures and the subsidies it provides indirectly through the tax system, which are sometimes referred to as **tax expenditures**. Direct expenditures comprise what the federal government spends on infrastructure (for example, by funding construction of dams and other water resources by the Army Corps of Engineers) and what it provides as grants and loan subsidies to states and localities (primarily for transportation projects). Those expenditures and grants account for a bit more than one-eighth of the roughly half-trillion dollars in total capital expenditures on infrastructure in the United States. However, for specific types of projects—for example, transportation and environmental facilities—those outlays represent about one-half or more of the total investment.

In: Role of Tax Preferences in Financial... ISBN: 978-1-61668-546-1
Editors: Michael D. Scott

Chapter 1

PRESENT LAW AND BACKGROUND RELATING TO STATE AND LOCAL GOVERNMENT BONDS

Joint Committee on Taxation

INTRODUCTION

The Subcommittee on Select Revenue Measures of the House Committee on Ways and Means has scheduled a public hearing for March 16, 2006, on State and local government bonds. This document,[1] prepared by the staff of the Joint Committee on Taxation, provides a description of the present law and background relating to State and local government bonds.

I. GENERAL OVERVIEW OF THE TAX SUBSIDY PROVIDED FOR STATE AND LOCAL BONDS

A. Tax-Exempt Bonds

In general

Interest on bonds issued by State and local governments generally is excluded from gross income for Federal income tax purposes. Bonds issued by State and local governments may be classified as either governmental bonds or private activity bonds. Governmental bonds are bonds the proceeds of which are primarily used to finance governmental functions or which are repaid with governmental funds. Private activity bonds are bonds in which the State or local government serves as a conduit providing financing to nongovernmental persons (e.g., private businesses or individuals). The exclusion from income for State and local bonds does not apply to private activity bonds, unless the bonds are issued for certain permitted purposes ("qualified private activity bonds") and other Code[2] requirements are met.

In addition to formally issuing bonds as evidence of indebtedness, State and local governments may undertake debt, the interest on which is tax-exempt, by means of installment sales contracts or finance leases. For example, a State or local government may purchase computers or other office equipment pursuant to a lease-purchase agreement or an ordinary written agreement of purchase and sale. Interest paid on such acquisitions is tax exempt if (1) the agreement calls for payment of the interest, and (2) the amounts are true interest (as opposed to other payments labeled as interest).[3] However, interest paid by State and local governments other than pursuant to the exercise of their borrowing power is not tax-exempt (e.g., interest on State income tax refunds).

Permitted Issuers

Qualified Governmental Units

Tax-exempt bonds must be issued by or on behalf of a State[4] or local government, or any political subdivision thereof ("qualified governmental units"). If bonds are issued directly by a State, city, or county, compliance with this requirement is easily determined; however, bonds often are issued by other entities that are not clearly political subdivisions of a State. For example, private activity bonds frequently are issued by entities with limited sovereign powers (e.g., an economic development authority). In such cases, the determination of whether the issuer is a political subdivision of the State may be less clear than in cases involving direct financings for local government operations. In general, an entity is a political subdivision (and thereby a qualified governmental unit) only if it has more than an insubstantial amount of one or more of the following governmental powers: the power to tax, the power of eminent domain, and the police power (in the law enforcement sense).[5]

On behalf of Entities

In addition to issuing bonds directly, State or local governments may establish other entities to issue bonds "on behalf of" such governmental units. These "on behalf of" corporations developed historically because some State laws and constitutions defined the purposes for which the State could issue bonds more narrowly than Federal tax law did. For example, qualified scholarship funding bonds are bonds issued by specially constituted nonprofit corporations acting on behalf of governmental units to facilitate the making of student loans.[6] Similarly, a nonprofit corporation might own, operate, and issue debt to finance a local airport. The general requirements that must be satisfied by these nonprofit corporations are specified in two administrative determinations of the Internal Revenue Service.[7]

Indian Tribal Governments

Although not States or subdivisions of States, Indian tribal governments are provided with a tax status similar to State and local governments for specified purposes under the Code.[8] Among the purposes for which a tribal government is treated as a State is the issuance of tax- exempt bonds. However, bonds issued by tribal governments are subject to limitations not imposed on State and local government issuers. Tribal governments are authorized to issue tax- exempt bonds only if substantially all of the proceeds are used for essential governmental functions or certain manufacturing facilities.[9]

Qualified Purposes

Governmental Bonds

Qualified governmental units generally may issue governmental bonds to finance general government operations and services, such as schools, courthouses, roads, and governmentally operated water, sewer, and electric facilities, without regard to most of the restrictions that apply to bonds used to finance private activities. For example, governmental bonds are not subject to issuance cost, maturity, and annual volume limitations that generally apply to qualified private activity bonds (see Part IV, below, for a general discussion of tax-exempt bond requirements).

Qualified Private Activity Bonds

In addition to issuing bonds for government operations and services, present law permits qualified governmental units to issue qualified private activity bonds to provide tax-exempt financing for certain private activities. In these cases, the qualified governmental unit generally acts as a conduit, that is, the qualified governmental unit issues the bonds, but the nongovernmental person[10] receiving the benefit of tax-exempt financing (the "conduit borrower") is the obligor on the bonds.

The definition of a qualified private activity bond includes an exempt facility bond,[11] or qualified mortgage, veterans' mortgage, small issue, redevelopment, 501(c)(3), or student loan bond.[12]

Present law also provides special rules for qualified private activity bonds issued within certain geographic areas (e.g., enterprise or empowerment zones, the New York Liberty Zone, and the Gulf Opportunity Zone) to provide incentives for businesses to locate in those areas.

The general requirements for qualified private activity bonds are discussed in Part IV, below.

Benefits and Cost of the Subsidy

Issuer Benefit

Tax-exempt financing provides a direct Federal subsidy to at least two parties to each transaction, the borrower (i.e., either the qualified governmental unit or the conduit borrower) and the bond investor (the lender). Because interest income on the bonds is excluded from gross income, the bond investor is willing to accept a lower rate on the bonds than he might otherwise accept on a taxable investment. Thus, the qualified issuer receives an implicit Federal subsidy equal to the difference between the tax-exempt interest rate paid and the taxable rate that otherwise would be paid. In this way, the income exclusion lowers the cost of capital for the State and local governments (or private parties in the case of private activity bonds).

The following example illustrates the Federal subsidy measured as a percentage of the otherwise applicable taxable rate. Assume a school district may borrow either at a taxable rate of 6.25 percent or a tax-exempt rate of 4.5 percent. The yield spread in this example is 1.75 percentage points and the ratio of tax-exempt to taxable rates is .72, or 72 percent, and the subsidy is equal to 28 percent of the otherwise applicable taxable rate.[13] To illustrate the benefit of the subsidy in dollar terms, if the school district borrows $1 million at the taxable rate of 6.25 percent and $1 million at the tax-exempt rate of 4.5

percent, the school district's annual interest payments would be $62,500 on the taxable debt, but $45,000 on the tax-exempt debt, a $17,500 savings. In practice, however, this calculation overstates the issuer's interest savings because of certain inefficiencies associated with the issuance of tax-exempt bonds (explained below).

Finally, as the ratio of tax-exempt rates to taxable debt rates moves closer to one (i.e., the spread between tax-exempt and taxable debt narrows), the value of the subsidy to the issuer also diminishes. Among other reasons, this may occur as the volume of tax-exempt bond issuances increases and tax-exempt issuers respond by offering higher interest rates to attract investors. (See Table 1 on page 7 comparing the average tax-exempt rate on high-grade municipal bonds and the average taxable rate on corporate bonds for the period 1986-2005).

Investor Benefit

The bond investor also receives a Federal subsidy from tax-exempt financing equal to the difference between the tax-exempt interest rate and the after-tax yield on a taxable investment. The investor's willingness to purchase tax-exempt bonds also depends on the investor's marginal tax rate. Generally, all other things being equal (such as credit worthiness), a taxpayer is indifferent between a tax-exempt bond and a taxable bond with an equivalent after-tax yield.[14] To illustrate using the example from above, if a taxpayer with a 28-percent marginal tax rate purchased a $1 million taxable bond at a 6.25-percent rate, as an alternative to the tax-exempt bond, he would receive $62,500 in interest income and pay $17,500 in income tax for a net return of $45,000 and an after-tax yield of 4.5 percent. This is the same net return the taxpayer receives if he were to purchase the $1 million tax-exempt bond. Thus, this investor generally would be indifferent to a taxable investment with a 6.25-percent rate and a tax-exempt investment with a 4.5-percent rate.

With many investors in different tax brackets, taxpayers in higher marginal tax-brackets receive a larger tax benefit than those in lower brackets. For example, if a taxpayer with a 33- percent marginal tax rate purchased the alternative $1 million taxable bond at a 6.25-percent rate, he would receive $62,500 in interest income and pay $20,625 in income tax for a net return of $41,875 and an after-tax yield of 4.19 percent. However, this taxpayer would receive a 4.5 percent net return on the school district's tax-exempt bond. Thus, unlike the taxpayer in the 28- percent marginal tax rate who is indifferent to investment in taxable or tax-exempt bonds, the taxpayer in the 33-percent marginal tax rate receives a greater benefit by purchasing the tax- exempt bond. In contrast, a taxpayer with a 15-percent marginal tax rate receives no benefit from purchasing the tax-exempt bond.

Revenue Loss Associated with Tax-Exempt Bonds

The direct cost to the Federal government of the interest exclusion for State and local bonds is the income tax revenue forgone. Under our example, if the taxpayer with a 28-percent marginal tax rate purchases the school district's $1 million tax-exempt bond with a 4.5-percent interest rate, the taxpayer receives $45,000 of tax-exempt interest income for each year the bond is outstanding. However, assuming the taxpayer's preferred alternative investment is a taxable bond, the actual revenue loss to the Federal government is based upon the taxable yield the taxpayer forgoes. For example, if the taxpayer purchased the taxable bond at a 6.25-percent rate, rather than the tax-exempt bond, he would have received $62,500 in interest income and paid $17,500 in income tax. In this case, the revenue forgone to the Federal Government equals the interest savings of the school district.

However, using the example from above, if the taxpayer in the 33-percent bracket purchases the school district's tax-exempt bond it costs the Federal Government $20,625 ($62,500 of interest income taxed at a 33-percent rate). Due to the existence of multiple tax brackets, the loss of Federal receipts is greater than the reduction in the tax-exempt issuer's interest savings. In this case, the $17,500 interest subsidy realized by the school district costs the Federal Government $20,625. The difference accrues to investors in tax brackets higher than those that would be implied by the yield spread between taxable and tax-exempt bonds. Thus, if a taxpayer in the 28-percent bracket finds it profitable to hold a tax-exempt security, a taxpayer in the 33-percent bracket will find it even more profitable. This implies that the Federal Government will lose more in revenue than the tax-exempt issuer gains in reduced interest payments. This is one source of inefficiency to the subsidy provided by the tax exemption.

Issuance Costs

Generally, issuing tax-exempt bonds to finance capital costs is a complex and expensive process. In addition to the issuer and investor, there are a number of parties employed to facilitate a bond issuance (e.g., investment bankers and attorneys). The requirements for tax exemption may result in higher incremental costs of issuance for tax-exempt bonds than those associated with issuing taxable bonds. Because a portion of the benefits of tax exemption flows to these intermediaries in the way of fees, such fees are a second potential source of inefficiency resulting from tax-exempt financing.

Table 1. Comparison of Taxable Interest Rates and Tax-Exempt Interest Rates, 1986-2005

Year	Corporate Bonds[1] [Percent]	High-Grade Municipal Bonds[1] [Percent]	Yield Spread	Implied Tax Rate of Marginal Holder [Percent]
1986	9.02	7.38	1.64	18
1987	9.38	7.73	1.65	18
1988	9.71	7.76	1.95	20
1989	9.26	7.24	2.02	22
1990	9.32	7.25	2.07	22
1991	8.77	6.89	1.88	21
1992	8.14	6.41	1.73	21
1993	7.22	5.63	1.59	22
1994	7.96	6.19	1.77	22
1995	7.59	5.95	1.64	22
1996	7.37	5.75	1.62	22
1997	7.26	5.55	1.71	24
1998	6.53	5.12	1.41	22
1999	7.04	5.43	1.61	23
2000	7.62	5.77	1.85	24
2001	7.08	5.19	1.89	27
2002	6.49	5.05	1.44	22
2003	5.67	4.73	0.94	17
2004	5.63	4.63	1.00	18
2005	5.24	4.29	1.05	18

[1] Annual average bond yield.
Source: Economic Report of the President, 2006, Table B-73.

Arbitrage Potential

The lower borrowing cost obtained through tax-exempt bonds provides the opportunity to earn arbitrage profits by investing tax-exempt bond proceeds in higher yielding investments, unless such transactions are restricted. Arbitrage transactions have no economic substance, but are made profitable solely through the ability to borrow at tax-exempt rates. If permitted to earn and retain arbitrage profits, issuers would have a substantial incentive to issue more bonds, to issue them earlier, and to leave them outstanding longer than necessary. From a Federal standpoint, arbitrage is an inefficient alternative to additional borrowing, because it is more costly to the Federal

Government in terms of forgone tax revenue than the additional borrowing that would be necessary to produce the same amount of proceeds.

As discussed in Part IV, C, below, present law generally restricts the ability of qualified governmental units and other parties to earn and retain arbitrage profits.

B. Tax-Credit Bonds

In General

As an alternative to traditional tax-exempt bonds, the Code permits three types of tax- credit bonds. States and local governments have the authority to issue qualified zone academy bonds ("QZABS"), clean renewable energy bonds ("CREBS"), and "Gulf tax credit bonds."[15] The specific requirements for QZABS, CREBS, and Gulf tax credit bonds are discussed in Part IV, C, below.

Tax-credit bonds are not interest-bearing obligations. Rather, the taxpayer holding a tax- credit bond on a credit allowance date is entitled to a tax credit. The amount of the credit is determined by multiplying the bond's credit rate by the face amount[16] on the holder's bond. For the present law categories of tax-credit bonds, the credit rate on the bonds is determined by the Secretary of the Treasury and is an estimate of the rate that permits issuance of such bonds without discount and interest cost to the qualified issuer. The credit is includible in gross income (as if it were an interest payment on the bond), and can be claimed against regular income tax liability and alternative minimum tax liability.

Description of the Subsidy

Under present law, the subsidy provided by tax-credit bonds is deeper than the subsidy for tax-exempt bonds. This is because (if the bonds are not issued at discount) the issuer of tax- credit bonds pays no interest, only principal.[17] The "interest" is paid by the Federal Government in the form of tax credits. Thus, the issuer theoretically has an interest-free loan. In comparison, issuers of tax-exempt bonds pay both interest and principal on such obligations albeit less interest than if the debt were taxable. As noted above, the Federal subsidy provided to issuers of tax-exempt bonds is limited to the difference between the tax-exempt interest rate paid and the taxable bond rate that otherwise would be paid.

Though called a tax credit, the Federal subsidy for tax-credit bonds is equivalent to the Federal Government directly paying the interest on a taxable bond issue on behalf of the State or local government benefiting from the bond proceeds.[18] To see this, consider any taxable bond that bears an interest rate of 10 percent. A thousand dollar bond would thus produce an interest payment of $100 annually. The owner of the bond that receives this payment would receive a net payment of $100 less the taxes owed on that interest. If the taxpayer were in the 28-percent Federal tax bracket, such taxpayer would receive $72 after Federal taxes. Regardless of whether the State government or the Federal Government pays the interest, the taxpayer receives the same net of tax return of $72. In the case of tax-credit bonds, no formal interest is paid by the Federal Government. Rather, a tax credit of $100 is allowed to be taken by the holder of the bond. In general, a $100 tax credit would be worth $100 to a taxpayer, provided that the taxpayer had at least $100 in tax liability. However, for tax-credit bonds, the $100 credit also has to be claimed as income. Claiming an additional $100 in income costs a taxpayer in the 28-percent tax bracket an additional $28 in income taxes, payable to the Federal Government. With the $100 tax credit that is ultimately claimed, the taxpayer nets $72 of interest income by holding the bond. The Federal Government loses $100 on the credit, but recoups $28 of that by the requirement that it be included in income, for a net cost of $72, which is exactly the net return to the taxpayer. If the Federal Government had simply agreed to pay the interest on behalf of the State or local government, both the Federal Government and the bondholder/taxpayer would be in the same situation. The Federal Government would make outlays of $100 in interest payments, but would recoup $28 of that in tax receipts, for a net budgetary cost of $72, as before. Similarly, the bondholder/taxpayer would receive a taxable $100 in interest, and would owe $28 in taxes, for a net gain of $72, as before. The State or local government also would be in the same situation in both cases.

QZABs, unlike interest-bearing State and local bonds, CREBs, and Gulf tax credit bonds, are not subject to the arbitrage or rebate requirements of the Code. The ability of issuers of QZABs to invest proceeds at unrestricted yields and retain the earnings from such investments, increases the subsidy available for qualified expenditures, as well as the repayment of principal on such bonds, beyond the savings achieved through having the issuer's interest costs paid by the Federal tax credit. Moreover, the ability to earn and retain arbitrage profits provides an incentive for issuers to issue more bonds and to issue them earlier than necessary. As a result, there may be increased delays in the expenditure of bond proceeds for approved purposes in order to earn greater arbitrage profits.[19]

Table 2 below provides an estimate of tax expenditures for governmental bonds, qualified private activity bonds and tax-credit bonds for fiscal years 2006-20 10.

II. Legislative History Relating to Private Use of State and Local Bond Proceeds

In general

Federal income tax law has provided an exclusion for interest on bonds issued by or on behalf of State and local governments since the income tax was enacted in 1913. Throughout most of the twentieth century, State and local bonds primarily were issued to finance public infrastructure projects, e.g., schools, roads, public utilities, and mass transit systems. Federal tax law at that time, however, did not distinguish between bonds issued for public as opposed to private purposes.[20]

The 1954 Tax Code (1954-1985)

In 1954, the Internal Revenue Service ruled favorably on the use of tax-exempt revenue bonds[21] to provide financing for private businesses.[22] However, the volume of tax-exempt bonds to provide financing for private business activities was relatively small until the 1960's. At that time, the volume of bonds for private activities began to grow rapidly.

In response to the increased volume of bonds issued for private activities, Congress, as part of the Revenue Adjustment Act of 1968 (the "1968 Act"),[23] enacted the first statutory provisions limiting the circumstances under which interest on such bonds would be tax exempt. Specifically, the 1968 Act provided that interest on industrial development bonds ("IDBs," the original private-activity bonds) generally is taxable. IDBs were defined as obligations: (1) more than 25 percent of the proceeds of which were to be used in a trade or business carried on by a nonexempt person (any person other than a governmental unit or a 501 (c)(3) organization), and (2) the payment of more than 25 percent of the principal or interest on which was to be derived from or secured by money or property used in a trade or business.

Table 2. Tax Expenditure, Total for 2006-2010 [Dollars in Billions]

Tax Exempt Bonds:	
Governmental Bonds	149.2
Private Activity Bonds (Total)	47.5
Select Categories of Private Activity Bonds by Purpose:	
Sewage Water, Waste	4.7
Airports, Docks and Mass Commuting	6.0
Nonprofit Health	11.9
Nonprofit Education	7.7
Rental Housing	1.7
Owner Occupied Housing	8.3
Tax Credit Bonds:	
Qualified Zone Academy Bonds ("QZABS")	2.1
Clean Renewable Energy Bonds ("CREBs")	0.2
Gulf Tax Credit Bonds	[less than 50 million]

Source: Joint Committee on Taxation.

Congress stated that the interest income on IDBs should be taxable because such bonds "were not 'obligations of a State or any political subdivision' within the meaning of section 103 since the primary obligor was not a State or political subdivision."[24] Exceptions were provided, however, in the form of a list of activities for which tax-exempt IDB financing could be provided[25] and a more general exception for certain small issues (the "small issue exception").

Although the 1968 Act imposed the first statutory restrictions on tax-exempt financing for private activities, it also left large exceptions to the prohibition and issuances continued to increase. In 1975, $8.9 billion of tax-exempt bonds for private activities were issued. By 1980, issuance had increased to $32.5 billion, or more than half the total tax-exempt market.[26] In addition, this period of time saw an increase in the volume of bonds issued to finance mortgage loans for single-family housing ("mortgage subsidy bonds"), which were not affected by the 1968 Act restrictions. State housing finance agencies began issuing mortgage subsidy bonds in the early 1970s and by 1980 the volume had grown to $10.5 billion. This increase in issuance volume led to the Mortgage Subsidy Act of 1980 (the "1980 Act").[27] The 1980 Act limited the tax exemption for mortgage subsidy bonds to two types, qualified veterans' mortgage bonds and qualified mortgage bonds (see Part IV, below, for present-law requirements). The 1980 Act also imposed a volume limitation on mortgage bonds, the first time such a limitation was imposed on a category of tax-exempt bonds.

With the continued expansion of the private activity bond market, in 1982, Congress imposed additional restrictions on such bonds. The changes to the private activity bond rules made by the Tax Equity and Fiscal Responsibility Act of 1982 ("TEFRA") included the following: (1) issuers of private activity bonds were required to make quarterly information reports to the IRS;[28] (2) issuance of IDBs was required to be approved by an elected official following a public hearing; and (3) the average length of time to maturity of IDBs was limited to 120 percent of the economic life of the property financed. Additionally, the small issue exception was to sunset at the end of 1986.[29]

By 1984, Congress was "extremely concerned with the volume of tax-exempt bonds used to finance private activities."[30] The volume of these bonds had increased to $62.4 billion in 1983, representing 68 percent of total State and local borrowings.[31] Moreover, Congress determined that the TEFRA rules enacted in 1982 appeared unlikely to impose adequate limits on the overall growth in the volume of private activity bonds. In response, the Deficit Reduction Act of 1984 (the "1984 Act")[32] imposed volume limitations on the aggregate annual amount of private activity bonds (most IDBs and all bonds issued to finance student loans) that could be issued by each State and its political subdivisions. The 1984 Act also provided that interest on bonds issued to provide loans to nonexempt persons is taxable. Private activity bonds for which Congress previously had authorized tax exemption (i.e., IDBs, mortgage subsidy bonds, and student loan bonds) were not subject to the private-loan restriction.

The 1984 Act also included provisions of general application to tax-exempt bonds, including bonds issued for private activities. For example, the 1984 Act generally prohibited tax exemption for interest on bonds that are guaranteed, in whole or in part, by a direct or indirect guarantee of the Federal Government.[33] Exceptions were provided for certain guarantee programs in existence when the 1984 Act was enacted. In addition, the 1984 Act provided that all future grants of exemption from Federal tax for bond interest must be enacted as part of a revenue act.

The Tax Reform Act of 1986

Between 1975 and 1985, the volume of long-term tax-exempt bonds issued for private activities (including tax-exempt IDBs, student loan bonds, mortgage bonds, and bonds issued for 501 (c)(3) organizations) increased from $8.9 billion to $116.4 billion.[34] As a share of total State and local government borrowings, financing for private activities increased from 29 percent to 53 percent. This increase in volume affected the efficiency and equity of the tax system in several ways.

First, the large volume of tax-exempt bonds issued for private activities increased the interest rates that State and local governments were required to pay to finance their activities. As the total volume of tax-exempt bonds increases, the interest rate on such bonds must increase to attract investment from competing sources, thus, increasing the cost of financing essential governmental services.

Second, tax-exempt financing for certain private activities may have resulted in a misallocation of capital. Efficient allocation of capital requires that the return from a marginal unit of investment be equal across activities. Tax-exempt bonds change the allocation of capital by encouraging investment in projects eligible for tax-exempt financing, at the expense of other investments. In certain cases, tax-exempt bonds may encourage investment in projects that serve little or no public purpose. For example, the availability of small issue financing may have encouraged small projects at the expense of larger ones, regardless of relative economic efficiency.[35]

Third, the growth of issuances for private activities raised concerns of fairness. Because of the large volume of tax-exempt obligations issued for private activities, tax-exempt yields were often close to taxable yields. Taxpayers with high marginal tax rates accordingly received an after-tax yield on tax-exempt bonds significantly higher than the yield they would have received from taxable investments. A perception of inequity arises when such investors are able to reduce their tax liability and still receive a rate of return nearly as high as that on taxable investments.

In response to these and other concerns, the Tax Reform Act of 1986 (the "1986 Act")[36] made significant changes to the rules regarding all tax-exempt bonds. The 1986 Act retained the tax-exemption for interest on State and local government bonds used to finance traditional government operations, but adopted new tests to restrict the diversion of governmental bond proceeds for private purposes not specifically authorized to receive tax-exempt financing. Specifically, the 1986 Act provided that a bond is not a tax-exempt bond if it is a private activity bond. The 1986 Act defined a private activity bonds as any bond that satisfies (1) the private business use test and the private security or payment test ("the private business test"); or (2) "the private loan financing test."[37] The private business test is a modified version of the two-part test used to define IDBs under prior law, but the thresholds for impermissible private use and private payments were tightened from 25 percent to 10 percent.

The 1986 Act continued many of the prior-law exceptions allowing tax-exempt financing for certain private activities. Under the 1986 Act, the definition of a tax-exempt, qualified private activity bond included: exempt facility bonds,[38] mortgage revenue bonds (including veterans' bonds), qualified 501(c)(3) bonds, qualified student loan bonds, qualified small-issue bonds, and qualified redevelopment bonds.[39] The 1986 Act eliminated sports facilities, convention and trade show facilities, parking facilities, private pollution control facilities, and industrial parks from the list of facilities eligible for tax-exempt financing. Eligibility was extended, however, to hazardous waste disposal facility bonds and qualified redevelopment bonds.

Prior law contained separate volume limitations for (1) IDBs and student loan bonds, (2) mortgage bonds, and (3) veterans' mortgage bonds. The 1986 Act provided a unified State annual volume limitation ("volume cap") for most qualified private activity bonds. The 1986 Act set the volume cap for each State at the greater of $50 per resident or $150 million per annum.[40] Qualified 501(c)(3) bonds and exempt facility bonds for governmentally owned airports, docks and wharves and governmentally owned solid waste disposal facilities were not subject to volume limitations under the 1986 Act.

Generally, the 1986 Act requires 95 percent of the net proceeds of qualified private activity bonds to be spent for the exempt purpose of the borrowing. The 1986 Act also limits the amount of costs of issuance that may be paid from most private activity bond proceeds to two percent and further provides that amounts paid for costs of issuance are not treated as spent for the exempt purpose of the borrowing (i.e., are not counted in determining whether the 95 percent requirement, etc. is satisfied).

The 1986 Act extended the public approval requirements that previously applied to IDBs to all private activity bonds. The maturity restrictions on IDBs were extended to qualified 501(c)(3) bonds under the 1986 Act, and qualified 501(c)(3) bonds (other than hospital bonds) were subject to a $150 million per institution limit on outstanding bonds.[41]

Post-1986 Act (1988-Present)

Expansion of Eligible Activities

The Technical and Miscellaneous Revenue Act of 1988[42] added high-speed intercity rail facilities to the list of activities eligible for tax-exempt financing.[43] Seventy-five percent of the principal amount of the bonds issued for high-speed rail facilities is exempt from the volume limit.[44] If all the property to be financed by the net proceeds of the issue is to be owned by a governmental unit, then such bonds are completely exempt from the volume limit.

The Energy Policy Act of 1992[45] added environmental enhancements of hydro-electric generating facilities to the list of exempt facility bonds. Eligible facilities include those that protect or promote fisheries or other wildlife resources and those for recreational purposes or other improvements required by the terms of a Federal license for the operation of a hydroelectric generating facilities. Bonds issued for these purposes are not subject to volume limitations.

The Omnibus Budget Reconciliation Act of 1993 (the "1993 Act") authorized the designation of a total of nine empowerment zones and 95 enterprise communities to provide tax incentives for businesses to locate within certain geographic areas designated by the Secretaries of Housing and Urban Development ("HUD") and Agriculture. The 1993 Act provided expanded tax-exempt financing for certain businesses in empowerment zones and enterprise communities.

The Tax Relief Act of 1997[46] authorized the issuance of qualified zone academy bonds ("QZABS"), the first type of tax-credit bond. A total of $400 million of QZABs was authorized to be issued annually in calendar years 1998 and 1999.[47]

The Economic Growth and Tax Reconciliation Act of 2001 ("EGTRA") added qualified public education facilities to the list of exempt facilities. Qualified public education facilities include elementary and secondary public school facilities which are owned by private, for-profit corporations pursuant to public-private partnership agreements with a State or local educational agency. Issuance of these bonds is subject to a separate annual per-State volume limit equal to $10 per resident (or $5 million, if greater) in lieu of the general State volume cap limits.

The Job Creation and Worker Assistance Act of 2002 ("JCWAA") authorized an aggregate of $8 billion in exempt facility bonds for the purpose of financing the construction and rehabilitation of nonresidential real property and residential rental real property in the New York Liberty Zone ("New York Liberty Zone Bonds").[48]

The American Jobs Creation Act of 2004[49] created a new category of exempt facility bond, the qualified green building and sustainable design project bond ("qualified green bond"). Generally, a qualified green bond is defined as any bond issued as part of an issue that finances a project designated by the Secretary, after consultation with the Administrator of the Environmental Protection Agency, as a green building and sustainable design project. Green bonds are not subject to the State bond volume cap. Rather, there is a national limitation of $2 billion of qualified green bond issuance authority that may be allocated to qualified green building and sustainable design projects. The authority to issue green bonds terminates after September 30, 2009.

The Safe, Accountable, Flexible, Efficient Transportation Equity Act: A Legacy for Users,[50] authorized new categories of exempt facility bonds to finance qualified highway or surface freight transfer facilities. Qualified highway or surface freight transfer facilities are not subject to the State volume cap. Rather, the Secretary of Transportation is authorized to allocate a total of $15 billion of issuance authority to qualified highway or surface freight transfer facilities.

The Energy Policy Act of 2005[51] authorized the second type of tax-credit bond, clean renewable energy bonds ("CREBs"), to finance the type of facilities that qualify for the tax credit under section 45. There is a national CREB limitation of $800 million that must be issued before December 31, 2007.

The Gulf Opportunity Zone Act of 2005[52] authorized both the third category of tax-credit bonds, Gulf tax credit bonds, and a new type of qualified private activity bond, Gulf Opportunity Zone Bonds. The maximum amount of Gulf tax credit bonds that may be issued is $200 million in the case of Louisiana, $100 million in the case of Mississippi, and $50 million in the case of Alabama. Gulf Opportunity Zone Bonds are not subject to the State volume cap. Rather, the volume on bonds that may be issued is based on the population of the three States that may issue such bonds, Alabama, Louisiana, or Mississippi, that resides within the Gulf Opportunity Zone.[53]

Increases in Volume Cap

In addition to expanding the types of private activities eligible for tax-exempt financing, Congress also has increased the State volume cap applicable to most categories of qualified private activity bonds.

The Omnibus Consolidated and Emergency Supplemental Appropriations Act, 1999[54] increased the annual volume cap that applies to private activity bonds to $75 per resident of each State or $225 million, if greater, beginning in calendar year 2007. The increase was to be, ratably phased in, beginning with $55 per capita or $165 million, if greater, in calendar year 2003.

The Community Renewal Tax Relief Act of 2000[55] accelerated the increase to the volume cap that was enacted in 1998. The State volume cap was increased to the greater of $62.50 per resident or $187.5 million in calendar year 2001, the greater of $75 per resident or $225 million in calendar year 2002, and, beginning in calendar year 2003, volume cap is adjusted annually for inflation.[56]

Since the volume cap limits have been increased, significant amounts of the State volume cap have been unused.[57] Table 3, below, shows both the allocated and unused volume cap amounts for the years 1998-2004.

III. Select Issues Related to Use of Tax-Exempt Bond and Tax-Credit Bond Proceeds

A. The Concept of Private Use of Governmental Bonds

Present law does not define the governmental or public purposes for which governmental bonds maybe issued. Rather, the Code defines a taxable private activity bond based on use of bond proceeds and the manner in which bonds are paid or secured. Congress adopted the private activity bond rules in response to concerns that a significant amount of proceeds from governmental bonds was being used to finance private activities.[58] The use of tax-exempt bond proceeds to finance private activities was viewed as an inefficient use of the Federal subsidy that increased the cost of financing traditional government activities.[59] The private activity bond rules enacted in the 1986 Act reflected the intent of Congress to restrict the diversion of governmental bond proceeds for private purposes not specifically authorized to receive tax- exempt financing.

Classification as a private activity bond can be avoided, however, by "failing" to meet either prong of the private business test: the private business use test or the private payment test.[60] By requiring that both the use and payment tests be met before a bond is a taxable private activity bond, the law permits the issuance of tax-exempt bonds to finance private activities in situations in which taxpayers, rather than the private party receiving the benefit of tax-exempt financing, are the obligors on the debt. As a result, present law permits the use of bond proceeds for private activities that Congress has not specifically approved to benefit from the indirect Federal subsidy provided through tax exemption if bonds are secured and paid by public funds (i.e., tax revenues).

For example, prior to the 1986 Act, the Code expressly allowed tax-exempt financing for sports facilities. The 1986 Act discontinued this express authority by eliminating sports facilities from the list of activities eligible for tax-exempt financing.[61] Municipalities, however, continue to subsidize sports facilities using tax-exempt bonds. This is because stadiums qualify for tax-exempt financing under present law even if the bonds providing such financing exceed either the 10-percent private business use test or the 10-percent private payment test, but not both. Use by a professional sports team almost always will cause the private business use test to be met, so a stadium bond must be structured so that debt service is primarily paid from sources other than stadium revenues or other private payments.[62] Because only one prong of the private business test is satisfied in such cases, the bonds are not treated as private activity bonds.[63] In effect, present law virtually requires that if a stadium is to be financed with tax-exempt bonds, a municipality must enter into an arrangement granting a professional sports team use of the stadium at substantially less than market value. This example is not unique to stadiums, however. Qualified governmental units may issue governmental bonds for any number of privately used facilities (e.g., corporate industrial parks and parking garages) if the debt service on the bonds is secured by public funds.

Present law also may provide issuers with an incentive to issue bonds as governmental rather than qualified private activity bonds, even when an activity may be financed with either type of bond. As described above, governmental bonds are not subject to volume cap and other limitations that apply to qualified private activity bonds.[64] In addition, investor demand may be greater for governmental bonds than qualified private activity bonds because the interest income on most qualified private activity bonds is subject to the alternative minimum tax ("AMT"),[65] whereas the interest income on governmental bonds is not. The preferential treatment afforded governmental bonds may have the effect of encouraging the commitment of public funds to certain activities to avoid the private business tests. In such a case, more of the benefit of tax- exempt financing is transferred to private parties, rather than to State or local governments, a result that is inconsistent with the purpose of the subsidy.

Table 3. Private Activity Bond Volume Cap and Carryforward [Dollars in Millions]

Year	Allocated[1]	Unused Cap[2] (Carryforwards)
1998	15,151	3,097
1999	15,271	3,346
2000	15,380	3,615
2001	19,704	6,684
2002	23,876	12,150
2003	24,198	17,346
2004	25,766	22,950

[1] Source: The Bond Buyer Yearbook.
[2] Source: The Bond Buyer.

B. Growth of Activities Eligible for Tax-Exempt Bonds and Attendant Increase in Volume Limits

While continuing tax-exempt financing for a number of private activities eligible under prior law, the 1986 Act reflected Congress' intent to control the volume of bonds issued for such activities. To accomplish this, the 1986 Act established the volume cap, rules provided to limit the aggregate annual volume of most qualified private activity bonds that each State (including local governments therein) may issue.[66] Moreover, the imposition of a single volume cap in 1986, in place of the separate limitations imposed on different categories of private activity bonds under prior law, was intended to allow State and local governments flexibility in allocating the limited Federal subsidy among qualifying activities.

In recent years, Congress has expanded the list of private activities eligible for tax-exempt financing. Including the preferential rules for certain geographic areas (e.g., enterprise zones, the New York Liberty Zone, and the Gulf Opportunity Zone), there are now 25 categories of private activities eligible for tax-exempt financing. Moreover, every type of private activity bond added to the Code since 1988 has been either wholly or partially excepted from the unified volume cap. Continued expansion of the types of private activities eligible for tax-exempt financing but excepted from volume cap limitations may result in the situation Congress attempted to address through the 1986 Act, i.e., increased amounts of bonds issued for private activities which had the effect of increasing the borrowing costs for all issuers of tax-exempt bonds because of competition for the limited pool of assets for investment in such obligations.

To constrain issuance volume, many of the recent categories of private activities are subject to separate volume limitations (e.g., green bonds, highway or surface freight transfer facility bonds, public education facilities).[67] However, separate volume limitations may result in inefficient allocations of capital because State and local governments are restricted in their ability to allocate the subsidy to projects that may provide the greatest benefit; precisely the situation Congress intended to eliminate when creating the unified volume cap.

Separate volume limitations for certain activities ensure that such activities receive a dedicated allocation of issuance authority. A unified volume cap may force projects to compete for limited allocations. Congress, however, has raised the volume cap limits and, under present law, the volume cap is now indexed for inflation. As a result of the increases in the State volume cap, most States have had unused issuance authority in recent years. With excess volume cap available to issuers, there is less need to provide separate volume limitations for certain activities.

Table 3, above, shows the national amount of volume cap that was allocated to private activity bonds and the amount of unused volume cap from 1998-2004.

In addition, the volume allocations with respect to certain categories of bonds (e.g., highway or surface freight transfer facility bonds) are made at the Federal level, rather than the local level. Historically, State and local governments have controlled the decision as to whether to provide financing for private activities within their jurisdiction. Allocating private activity bond issuance authority at the Federal level removes the element of local control and may force State and local governments to directly compete with private businesses to raise capital.

Although present law does not impose a "public purpose" requirement on qualified private activity bonds, many of the original activities eligible for tax-exempt financing under the 1986 Act perform essentially public functions (e.g., airports, docks and wharves, solid waste facilities). As the benefit of tax-exempt financing is extended to additional, but narrower, categories of private activities it becomes more difficult to identify the public purpose served by such activities. To the extent tax-exempt financing is provided for narrowly defined business activities, there may be little or no public benefit provided by such activities. While some suggest that increases in employment and expansion of the local tax base are public activities of sufficient importance to justify subsidized financing for private activities, others respond that expanding the use of tax-exempt bonds for private activities has anti-competitive and distortive effects on the economy. Parties eligible for subsidized financing receive a significant advantage over their competitors, which must raise capital with higher-cost taxable obligations. Moreover, tax-exempt financing changes the allocation of capital by encouraging investment in projects eligible for such financing, at the expense of other investments, regardless of the relative economic efficiencies of the competing investments.

See Figure 1, page 25, for a comparison of the annual issuance volume of long-term governmental bonds and long-term qualified private activity bonds for the period 1993-2003.

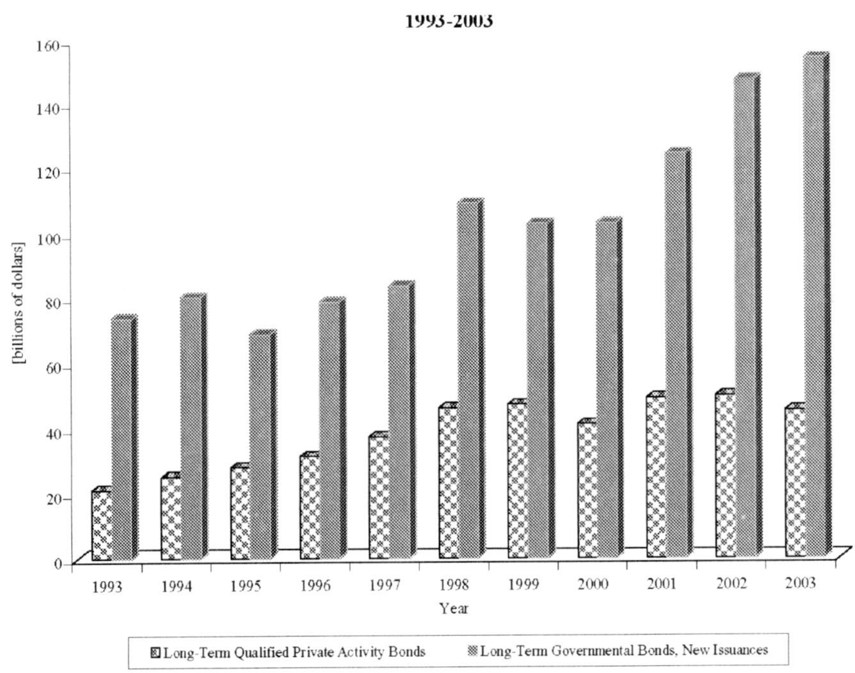

Note: *Issues of long-term bonds.

Figure 1. Annual Issuance of Tax-Exempt Governmental and Private Activity Bonds,* 1993-2003

C. Use of Tax-Credit Bond Proceeds as an Alternative to Tax-Exempt Bonds

Like tax-exempt bonds, tax-credit bonds operate to lower the borrowing costs of eligible borrowers. Tax-credit bonds also raise many of the same issues as tax-exempt bonds. For example, parties eligible for tax-credit bond financing receive a significant advantage over their competitors. Similarly, tax-credit bonds encourage investment in projects eligible for such financing, at the expense of other investments.

Expansion of Permitted Issuers beyond State and Local Governments

Historically, the subsidy provided by tax-exempt financing has been limited to obligations issued by qualified governmental units, i.e., States or local governments, or any political subdivisions thereof. However, under present law, CREBs may be issued by certain cooperative lenders and electric companies, in addition to qualified governmental units. Moreover, some have advocated expansion of this approach, i.e., permitting nongovernmental, private entities to issue tax-credit bonds for an expanded list of activities. Permitting nongovernmental entities to issue tax-exempt or tax-credit bonds represents a significant change in tax policy. As discussed above, present law subsidizes the activities of State and local governments in order to reduce the borrowing costs of such entities. In addition, present law limits financing for private activities because of the potential effect such financings have on the cost of capital for traditional public infrastructure projects, i.e., higher interest rates on tax-exempt bonds generally as competition increases for the limited pool of assets available for investment in tax-exempt obligations generally. Permitting nongovernmental parties to issue tax-subsidized obligations (whether as tax-exempt or tax-credit bonds) exacerbates that problem because, in addition to the increased volume of financing for private activities that may not serve a public purpose, governmental units lose the ability to determine the projects within their jurisdiction that should receive the benefit of subsidized financing.[68] As discussed, State and local governments traditionally have controlled the decisions of whether to provide financing for private activities. In contrast, permitting nongovernmental persons to directly issue bonds for private activities will force governmental units financing public projects to compete with these private entities to raise capital.[69]

Arbitrage

QZABs, unlike interest-bearing State and local bonds, CREBs, and Gulf tax credit bonds, are not subject to the arbitrage or rebate requirements of the Code. The ability of issuers of QZABs to invest proceeds at unrestricted yields and retain the arbitrage earnings from such investments increases the subsidy available for qualified expenditures, as well as the repayment of principal on such bonds, beyond the savings achieved through having the issuer's interest costs paid by the Federal tax credit. Moreover, the ability to earn and retain arbitrage profits provides an incentive for issuers to issue more bonds and to issue them earlier than necessary. As a result, there may be increased delays in the expenditure of bond proceeds for approved purposes in order to earn greater arbitrage profits.[70]

IV. Present-Law Requirements Related to Use of Tax-Exempt and Tax-Credit Bond Proceeds

A. Governmental Bonds

In General

Whether bonds are governmental bonds is not determined by the type of facility financed, but rather the use of the bond proceeds and the manner in which the bonds are paid or secured. The Code also does not define a governmental bond, but rather defines an impermissible private activity bond, i.e., a bond that is not a governmental bond. The Code defines a private activity bond as any bond that satisfies (1) the private business use test and the private security or payment test ("the private business test"); or (2) "the private loan financing test."[71] Generally, private activity bonds are taxable unless issued as qualified private activity bonds.

Private Activity Bond Tests

Two-Part Private Business Test

Under the private business test, a bond is a private activity bond if it is part of an issue in which:

1. More than 10 percent of the proceeds of the issue (including use of the bond-financed property) are to be used in the trade or business of any person other than a governmental unit ("private business use"); and
2. More than 10 percent of the payment of principal or interest on the issue is, directly or indirectly, secured by (a) property used or to be used for a private business use or (b) to be derived from payments in respect of property, or borrowed money, used or to be used for a private business use ("private payment test").[72]

A bond is not a private activity bond unless both parts of the private business test (i.e., the private business use test and the private payment test) are met. Thus, a facility that is 100 percent privately used does not cause the bonds financing such facility to be private activity bonds if the bonds are not secured by or paid with private payments. For example, a stadium that will be used by a professional sports team may be financed with governmental bonds if the team, or other private party, does not pay the debt service on such bonds.

A contract between a private management or other service company and a governmental unit to operate bond-financed governmental facilities may result in private business use depending on the terms of the contract.[73] In general, a management contract gives rise to private business use if the compensation under the contract is based on net profits. Contracts for service incidental to the facility's primary functions, such as janitorial, office equipment repair and similar services, are not considered management contracts. Certain contracts involving hospital- admitting privileges, operation of public utility property, and expense reimbursements are not treated as management contracts.

For purposes of the private payment test, both direct and indirect payments made by any private person treated as using the financed property are taken into account. Payments by a person for the use of proceeds generally do not include payments for ordinary and necessary expenses (within the meaning of section 162) attributable to the operation and maintenance of financed property.[74]

Private Loan Financing Test

A bond issue satisfies the private loan financing test if proceeds exceeding the lesser of $5 million or five percent of such proceeds are used directly or indirectly to finance loans to one or more nongovernmental persons. Private loans include both business and other (e.g., personal) uses and payments by private persons; however, in the case of business uses and payments, all private loans also constitute private business uses and payments subject to the private business test.

B. Qualified Private Activity Bonds

In General

Qualified private activity bonds are tax-exempt bonds issued to provide financing for specified privately used facilities.[75] Generally, qualified private activity bonds are subject to a number of restrictions that do not apply to governmental bonds, such as issuance cost, maturity, and annual volume limitations. In addition, the interest income from qualified private activity bonds (other than qualified 501 (c)(3) bonds) issued after August 7, 1986, is a preference item for purposes of calculating the alternative minimum tax ("AMT").[76]

Exempt Facility Bonds

The definition of a qualified private activity bond includes "exempt facility bonds." To qualify as an exempt facility bond, 95 percent of the net proceeds must be used to finance an eligible facility.[77] Business facilities eligible for this financing include transportation (airports, ports, local mass commuting, high-speed intercity rail facilities, and qualified highway or surface freight transfer facilities); privately owned and/or operated public works facilities (sewage, solid waste disposal, water, local district heating or cooling, and hazardous waste disposal facilities); privately-owned and/or operated residential rental housing; and certain private facilities for the local furnishing of electricity or gas. Bonds issued to finance "environmental enhancements of hydro-electric generating facilities," qualified public educational facilities, and qualified green building and sustainable design projects also may qualify as exempt facility bonds.

Residential rental projects are one of the more common types of projects financed with exempt-facility bonds. Residential rental property may be financed with exempt-facility bonds if the financed project is a "qualified residential rental project." A project is a qualified residential rental project if 20 percent or more of the residential units in such project are occupied by individuals whose income is 50 percent or less of area median gross income (the "20-50 test"). Alternatively, a project is a qualified residential rental project if 40 percent or more of the residential units in such project are occupied by individuals whose income is 60 percent or less of area median gross income (the "40-60 test").

Qualified Mortgage Bonds

Owner-occupied housing may be financed with qualified mortgage bonds. Qualified mortgage bonds are bonds issued to make mortgage loans to qualified mortgagors for the purchase, improvement, or rehabilitation of owner-occupied residences. The Code imposes several limitations on qualified mortgage bonds, including income limitations for homebuyers and purchase price limitations for the home financed with bond proceeds. The income limitations are satisfied if all financing provided by an issue is provided for mortgagors whose family income does not exceed 115 percent of the median family income for the metropolitan area or State, whichever is greater, in which the financed residences are located. The purchase price limitations provide that a residence financed with qualified mortgage bonds may not have a purchase price in excess of 90 percent of the average area purchase price for that residence. In addition to these limitations, qualified mortgage bonds generally cannot be used to finance a mortgage for a homebuyer who had an ownership interest in a principal residence in the three years preceding the execution of the mortgage (the "first-time homebuyer" requirement).[78]

Special income and purchase price limitations apply to targeted area residences. A targeted area residence is one located in either (1) a census tract in which at least 70 percent of the families have an income which is 80 percent or less of the State-wide median income or (2) an area of chronic economic distress. For targeted area residences, the income limitation is satisfied when no more than one-third of the mortgages are made without regard to any income limits and the remainder of the mortgages are made to mortgagors whose family income is 140 percent or less of the applicable median family income. The purchase price limitation is raised from 90 percent to 110 percent of the average area purchase price for targeted area residences. In addition, the first-time homebuyer requirement does not apply to targeted area residences.

Qualified mortgage bonds also may be used to finance qualified home-improvement loans. Qualified home-improvement loans are defined as loans to finance alterations, repairs, and improvements on an existing residence, but only if such alterations, repairs, and improvements substantially protect or improve the basic livability or energy efficiency of the property. Generally, qualified home-improvement loans may not exceed $15,000.

Qualified Veterans' Mortgage Bonds

Qualified veterans' mortgage bonds are bonds the proceeds of which are used to finance the purchase, or qualifying rehabilitation or improvement, of single-family, owner-occupied residences of qualified veterans located within the jurisdiction of the issuer of the bonds. A qualified veterans' mortgage bond may be issued only by those States that issued such bonds before June 22, 1984. These States are Alaska, California, Oregon, Texas, and Wisconsin. Annual issuance of qualified veterans' mortgage bonds is subject to a separate State limit, but not to the unified State volume cap applicable to most other private activity bonds.

Persons receiving qualified veterans' mortgage bond loans must be veterans who served on active duty at some time before January 1, 1977, and who applied for the financing before the later of the date 30 years after the last date on which the borrower left active service, or January 31, 1985. There are no restrictions on purchase price or borrower income, and no first-time homebuyer requirement for qualified veterans' mortgage bond loans.

Student Loan Bonds

Qualified student loan bonds are bonds issued to finance eligible student loans. Interest on qualified student loan bonds is tax-exempt. Eligible student loans include Federally guaranteed loans under the Higher Education Act of 1965 and other loans financed as part of a program of general application approved by the State.[79]

Small Issue Bonds

Qualified small issue bonds are tax-exempt bonds issued by State and local governments to finance private business manufacturing facilities (including certain directly related and ancillary facilities) or the acquisition of land and equipment by certain farmers. In both instances, these bonds are subject to limits on the amount of financing that may be provided, both for a single borrowing and in the aggregate. In general, no more than $1 million of small- issue bond financing may be outstanding at any time for property of a business (including related parties) located in the same municipality or county. Generally, this $1 million limit may be increased to $10 million if, in addition to outstanding bonds, all other capital expenditures of the business (including related parties) in the same municipality or county are counted toward the limit over a six-year period that begins three years before the issue date of the bonds and ends three years after such date. Outstanding aggregate borrowing is limited to $40 million per borrower (including related parties) regardless of where the property is located.

For bonds issued after September 30, 2009, the Code permits up to $10 million of capital expenditures to be disregarded, in effect increasing from $10 million to $20 million the maximum allowable amount of total capital expenditures by an eligible business in the same municipality or county.[80] However, no more than $10 million of bond financing may be outstanding at any time for property of an eligible business (including related parties) located in the same municipality or county. Other limits (e.g., the $40 million per borrower limit) also continue to apply.

Redevelopment Bonds

Qualified redevelopment bonds are bonds issued as part of an issue 95-percent or more of the net proceeds of which is to be used for one or more redevelopment purposes in a designated "blighted area." A blighted area is an area designated as such by the local governing body of such area based on the substantial presence of factors such as excessive vacant, abandoned or vacant buildings, substandard structures, vacancies, and delinquencies in payment of real property taxes.

Qualified redevelopment bonds must be issued pursuant to state law authorization and under an existing redevelopment plan. The payment of interest and principal on the issue must be financed, in effect, by taxes of general application or earmarked real estate tax increases. In addition, each real property interest in the designated blighted area that is acquired by a governmental unit and transferred to a nongovernmental person must be transferred for fair market value. No owner or user of property located in the financed area can be subject to a charge or fee which similarly situated owners or users of comparable property outside such area are not subject.

Qualified 501(c)(3) Bonds

State and local governments may issue tax-exempt bonds to finance the activities of charitable organizations described in section 501 (c)(3) ("qualified 501 (c)(3) bonds"). The beneficiaries of this type of financing frequently are private, nonprofit hospitals and private, nonprofit colleges and universities. Both capital expenditures and limited working capital expenditures of charitable organizations described in section 501 (c)(3) of the Code may be financed with qualified 501(c)(3) bonds.

Qualified 501(c)(3) bonds are not subject to the State volume cap.

New York Liberty Zone Bonds

Present law permits an aggregate of $8 billion in exempt facility bonds for the purpose of financing the construction and rehabilitation of nonresidential real property and residential rental real property in a designated "Liberty Zone" (the "Zone") of New York City ("Liberty Zone bonds"). The Zone consists of all business addresses located on or south of Canal Street, East Broadway (east of its intersection with Canal Street), or Grand Street (east of its intersection with East Broadway) in the Borough of Manhattan.

Property eligible for financing with these bonds includes buildings and their structural components, fixed tenant improvements, and public utility property (e.g., gas, water, electric, and telecommunication lines). Fixtures and equipment that could be removed from the designated zone for use elsewhere are not eligible for financing with these bonds. Issuance of these bonds is limited to projects approved by the Mayor of New York City or the Governor of New York State, each of whom may designate up to $4 billion of the aggregate bond authority.

Liberty Zone Bonds must be issued before January 1, 2010, and are not subject to the State volume cap.

Gulf Opportunity Zone Bonds

Present law permits the issuance of qualified private activity bonds to finance the construction and rehabilitation of residential and nonresidential property located in the Gulf Opportunity Zone ("Gulf Opportunity Zone Bonds").[81] Gulf Opportunity Zone Bonds must be issued before January 1, 2011.

Gulf Opportunity Zone Bonds may be issued by the State of Alabama, Louisiana, or Mississippi, or any political subdivision thereof. Gulf Opportunity Zone Bonds are not subject to the State volume cap. Rather, the maximum aggregate face amount of Gulf Opportunity Zone Bonds that may be issued in any State is limited to $2,500 multiplied by the population of the respective State within the Gulf Opportunity Zone. Depending on the purpose for which such bonds are issued, Gulf Opportunity Zone Bonds are treated as either exempt facility bonds or qualified mortgage bonds.

Gulf Opportunity Zone Bonds are treated as exempt facility bonds if 95 percent or more of the net proceeds of such bonds are to be used for qualified project costs located in the Gulf Opportunity Zone. Qualified project costs include the cost of acquisition, construction, reconstruction, and renovation of nonresidential real property, qualified residential rental projects (as defined in section 142(d) with certain modifications), and public utility property.

Gulf Opportunity Zone Bonds are treated as qualified mortgage bonds if the bonds of such issue meet the general requirements of a qualified mortgage issue and the residences financed with such bonds are located in the Gulf Opportunity Zone. For these residences the first-time homebuyer rule is waived and purchase and income rules for targeted area residences apply. In addition, 100 percent of the mortgages must be made to mortgagors whose family income is 140 percent or less of the applicable median family income.

Tax-Exempt Enterprise Zone Facility Bonds

Enterprise zone facility bonds are issued to finance "enterprise zone facilities" located in "enterprise communities" or "empowerment zones"[82] if the principal users of such facilities are "qualified enterprise zone businesses." Ninety-five percent or more of the net proceeds of the bonds must be used to provide an enterprise zone facility. An enterprise zone facility is defined as any qualified zone property the principal user of which is an "enterprise zone business," and any land that is functionally related and subordinate to such property.[83] Enterprise zone businesses are defined as certain partnerships or corporations conducting a qualified business in, and employing residents of, an empowerment zone.[84]

Additional Qualified Private Activity Bonds Requirements

Volume Cap

Unlike governmental bonds, the aggregate volume of most qualified private activity bonds is restricted by the annual volume cap imposed on issuers within each State.[85] As discussed above, the volume cap rules reflect Congress' intent to control the total volume of tax- exempt bonds issued for private activities.

For calendar year 2006, these annual volume limits, which are indexed for inflation, equal $80 per resident of the State, or $246,610,000 million, if greater.

Exceptions from the volume cap are provided for bonds for certain governmentally owned facilities (e.g., airports, ports, high-speed intercity rail, and solid waste disposal) and bonds issued to finance the activities of certain charitable organizations. In addition, bonds which are subject to separate local, State, or national volume limits are not subject to the unified volume cap (e.g., public/private educational facility bonds, enterprise zone facility bonds, qualified green building bonds, and qualified highway or surface freight transfer facility bonds).

If an issuer's volume cap for a calendar year exceeds the aggregate amount of tax-exempt private activity bonds issued during the year, the authority may elect to treat all (or any portion) of the excess as a carryforward for one or more specified "carryforward purposes." The issuing authority is required to identify the purpose for which the carryforward is elected and specify the portion of the carryforward which is to be used for that purpose. The Code defines "carryforward purpose" to mean one of four purposes: issuing exempt facility bonds; issuing qualified mortgage bonds or mortgage credit certificates; issuing qualified student loan bonds; and issuing qualified redevelopment bonds.[86] Carryforwards of unused volume cap are valid for three years.

Maturity Limitations

Most qualified private activity bonds are subject to a term to maturity rule which limits the period of time such bonds may remain outstanding. Generally, this rule provides that the average maturity of a qualified private activity bond cannot exceed 120 percent of the economic life of the property being financed.[87] The term to maturity rule does not apply to qualified mortgage or student loan bonds.[88]

Issuance Costs

Generally, the amount of costs of issuance (e.g., bond counsel and underwriter fees) that may be paid from qualified private activity bond proceeds is limited to two percent. In addition, amounts paid for costs of issuance are not treated as spent for the exempt purpose of the borrowing (i.e., are not "good costs").

Public Approval

To be a qualified private activity bond, a bond must satisfy a public approval requirement including providing reasonable public notice for a hearing. Regardless of State and local law, reasonable public notice must include notice "published in one or more newspapers of general circulation available to residents of that locality or if announced by radio or television broadcast to those residents."[89]

Prohibited Facilities

Qualified private activity bonds generally are subject to restrictions on the use of proceeds for the acquisition of land and existing property, use of proceeds to finance certain specified facilities (e.g., airplanes, skyboxes, other luxury boxes, health club facilities, gambling facilities, and liquor stores), and use of proceeds to pay costs of issuance. Small-issue and redevelopment bonds also are subject to additional restrictions on the use of proceeds for certain facilities (e.g., golf courses and massage parlors).

C. Rules Applicable to All Tax-Exempt Bonds

Arbitrage Restrictions

To prevent the issuance of more Federally subsidized tax-exempt bonds than necessary, the tax exemption for State and local bonds does not apply to any arbitrage bond.[90] An arbitrage bond is defined as any bond that is part of an issue if any proceeds of the issue are reasonably expected to be used (or intentionally are used) to acquire higher yielding investments or to replace funds that are used to acquire higher yielding investments. In general, arbitrage profits may be earned only during specified periods (e.g., defined "temporary periods") before funds are needed for the purpose of the borrowing or on specified types of investments (e.g., "reasonably required reserve or replacement funds"). Subject to limited exceptions, investment profits that are earned during these periods or on such investments must be rebated to the Federal Government ("arbitrage rebate").

Advance Refundings

A refunding bond is defined as any bond used to pay principal, interest, or redemption price on a prior bond issue (the refunded bond). The Code contains different rules for "current" as opposed to advance refunding bonds. A current refunding occurs when the refunded bond is redeemed within 90 days of issuance of the refunding bonds. Conversely, a bond is classified as an advance refunding if it is issued more than 90 days before the redemption of the refunded bond (thus, two or more issues of tax-exempt bonds are outstanding simultaneously).[91] Proceeds of advance refunding bonds are generally invested in an escrow account and held until a future date when the refunded bond may be redeemed.

Although there is no statutory limitation on the number of times that tax-exempt bonds may be currently refunded, the Code limits advance refundings. Generally, governmental bonds and qualified 501(c)(3) bonds may be advance refunded one time.[92] Private activity bonds, other than qualified 501(c)(3) bonds, may not be advance refunded at all.[93]

Federal Guarantees

Generally, interest on State and local bonds that are Federally guaranteed does not qualify for tax exemption. A bond is Federally guaranteed if: (1) the payment of principal or interest with respect to such bond is guaranteed (in whole or in part) by the United States (or any agency or instrumentality thereof); (2) such bond is issued as part of an issue and five percent of more of the proceeds of such issue is to be (a) used in making loans the payment of principal or interest with respect to which is guaranteed (in whole or in part) by the United States (or any agency or instrumentality thereof), or (b) invested directly or indirectly in federally insured deposits or accounts; or (3) the payment of principal or interest on such bond is otherwise indirectly guaranteed (in whole or in part) by the United States (or any agency or instrumentality thereof).

The Federal guarantee restriction was enacted in 1984 with certain exceptions for certain guarantee programs in existence at that time.[94]

Information Returns

An issuer of bonds must file with the IRS certain information in order for the interest on such bond to be tax-exempt.[95] Generally, this information return is required to be filed no later the 15th day of the second month after the close of the calendar quarter in which the bonds were issued.

D. Tax-Credit Bonds

In General

The three types of tax-credit bonds authorized under present law are QZABs, CREBs, and Gulf tax credit bonds.[96] A common feature of the three types of bonds is that the taxpayer holding a tax-credit bond on certain dates receives a tax credit, rather than interest. The amount of the credit is determined by multiplying the bond's credit rate by the face amount on the taxpayer's bond. The credit rate on the bonds is determined by the Secretary and is to be a rate that permits issuance of such bonds without discount and interest cost to the qualified issuer. The credit is includible in gross income (as if it were an interest payment on the bond), and can be claimed against regular income tax liability and alternative minimum tax liability. The specific requirements for each category of tax-credit bond is described below.

QZABs (Qualified Zone Academy Bonds)

QZABs are defined as any bond issued by a State or local government, provided that (1) at least 95 percent of the proceeds are used for the purpose of renovating, providing equipment to, developing course materials for use at, or training teachers and other school personnel in a "qualified zone academy," and (2) private entities have promised to contribute to the qualified zone academy certain equipment, technical assistance or training, employee services, or other property or services with a value equal to at least 10 percent of the bond proceeds.

A school is a "qualified zone academy" if (1) the school is a public school that provides education and training below the college level, (2) the school operates a special academic program in cooperation with businesses to enhance the academic curriculum and increase graduation and employment rates, and (3) either (a) the school is located in an empowerment zone or enterprise community designated under the Code, or (b) it is reasonably expected that at least 35 percent of the students at the school will be eligible for free or reduced-cost lunches under the school lunch program established under the National School Lunch Act.

A total of $400 million of QZABs was authorized to be issued annually in calendar years 1998 through 2005. The $400 million aggregate bond cap is allocated to the States according to their respective populations of individuals below the poverty line. Each State, in turn, allocates the credit authority to qualified zone academies within such State. Eligible holders of QZABs are limited to financial institutions.

Unlike issuers of tax-exempt bonds, issuers of QZABs are not required to file information returns with the Treasury. Moreover, such bonds are not subject to the general private use or arbitrage restrictions.

Clean Renewable Energy Bonds

CREBs are defined as any bond issued by a qualified issuer if, in addition to the requirements discussed below, 95 percent or more of the proceeds of such bonds are used to finance capital expenditures incurred by qualified borrowers for facilities that qualify for the tax credit under section 45 ("qualified projects" other than Indian coal production facilities), without regard to the placed-in-service date requirements of that section. There is a national CREB limitation of $800 millions. CREBs must be issued before December 31, 2007.

Unlike QZABs, CREBs are subject to the arbitrage requirements of section 148 that apply to tax-exempt bonds. In addition, to qualify as CREBs, generally, the qualified issuer must reasonably expect to and actually spend 95 percent or more of the proceeds of such bonds on qualified projects within the five-year period that begins on the date of issuance.

Unlike QZABs, issuers of CREBs are required to report issuance to the IRS in a manner similar to the information returns required for tax-exempt bonds.

Table 4. Categories of Qualified Private Activity Bonds

Eligible Facility	Purpose	Code Authorized	Subject to General Private Activity Bond Volume Cap
1. Airports (sec. 142(a)(1))	Airport terminals, runways, etc. (but not hotels, retail facilities, and offices if used in a private business).	1968	No
2. Docks and wharves (sec. 142(a)(2))	Private docks and wharves, including structures and equip-ment needed to disch-arge cargo and passe-ngers.	1968	No
3. Mass comm-uting facilities (sec. 142(a)(3))	Property serving bus, subway, rail, ferry, or other commuters on a day- to-day basis.	1968	Yes
4. Sewage facilities (sec. 142(a)(4))	Property used for cert-ain levels of treatment of wastewater and Property used for collection, storage, use, processing, or final disposal of wastewater, sewage, septage.	1968	Yes

Table 4 (continued)

5. Water facilities (sec. 142(a)(5))	Facilities furnishing water that is made available to the general public, including electric utility, industrial, agricultural, or other commercial users. Such facilities must be operated by a governmental unit or the rates for sale of water must be appro-ved by a governmental unit.	1968	Yes
6. Solid waste disposal faci-lities (sec. 142(a)(6))	Property used for the collection, storage, treatment, utilization, processing, or final disposal of solid waste.	1968	Yes, unless all property to be financed by the net proceeds of the issue is to be owned by a gove-rnmental unit.
7. Residential rental projects (sec. 142(a)(7))	A residential rental project in which 20 percent or more of the residential units are occupied by individu-als whose income is 50 percent or less of area median gross inc-ome or 40 percent or more of the residential units are occupied by	1968	Yes

	individuals whose inc-ome is 60 percent or less of area median gross income.		
8. Facilities for the local furnishing of electric energy or gas (sec. 142(a)(8))	Generally, a facility furnishing electric en-ergy or gas serving an area not exceeding two contiguous coun-ties or a city and one contiguous county.	1968	Yes
9. Qualified small issues (sec. 144(a))	Certain manufacturing facilities or the acquisition of land and equipment by certain farmers.	1968	Yes
10. Qualified 501(c)(3) property (sec. 145)	Capital expenditures and limited working capital expenditures of charitable organiz-ations described in section 501(c)(3),	1968	No
11. Qualified student loans (sec. 144(b))	Financing of student loans guaranteed un-der the Higher Education Act of 1965 and other loans financed as part of a program of general application approved by the State.	1976	Yes

Table 4 (continued)

12. Qualified mortgages (sec. 143(a))	Financing of mortgages for individuals meeting certain income, purchase price, and home-ownership requirements.	1980	Yes
13. Qualified veterans' mort-gages (sec. 143(a))	Financing of mortg-ages for veterans ser-ving prior to January 1, 1977, and applying for such a mortgage within 30 years of leaving active service. The only States that may issue bonds for this purpose are those States that had prog-rams in effect before June 22, 1984.	1980	No. Annual issu-ance is subject to a separate State limit based on the average amount of bonds issued for such purposes from January 1, 1979, through June 22, 1984.
14. Local dist-rict heating or cooling faci-lities (sec. 142(a)(9))	A facility providing hot water, chilled wa-ter, or steam to two or more users for resid-ential, commercial, or industrial heating or cooling, or process steam.	1982	Yes
15. Qualified hazardous waste facilities (sec. 142(a)(10))	Facilities for the inci-neration or permanent entombment of hazar-dous waste generated by the public.	1986	Yes
16. Qualified redevelopment purposes (sec. 144(c))	Financing of redevel-oppment in a locally designated "blighted area."	1986	Yes
17. High-speed intercity rail facilities (sec. 142(a)(11))	Facilities providing rail transportation of passengers and their baggage that uses vehicles that are reason-nably expected to operate at speeds in excess of 150 miles per hour between scheduled stops.	1988	No, if all prop-erty to be finan-ced by the net proceeds of the issue is to be owned by a governmental unit. Otherwise, 75 percent of the principal amount is exempt from the volume cap.

18. Environm-ental enhance-ments of hydro-electric generating facilities (sec. 142(a)(12))	Eligible facilities incl-ude those that protect or promote fisheries or other wildlife resources and those for recreational purposes or other improvements required by the terms of a Federal license for the operation of a hydro-electric generating facilities.	1992	No
19. Enterprise zones (sec. 1394)	Financing for certain "enterprise zone bus-inesses" which are de-fined as certain partn-erships or corporat-ions conducting a qualified business in, and employing residents of, an empowerment zone.	1993	Yes, unless issu-ed with respect to certain empower-ment zones.
20. Qualified public education facilities (sec. 142(a)(13))	Elementary and secondary public school facilities which are owned by private, for-profit corporations pursuant to public-private partnership agreements with a State or local educati-onnal agency.	2001	No. Subject to a separate annual per-State volume limit equal to $10 per resident (or $5 million, if gre-ater) in lieu of the general State vol-ume cap limits.
21. New York Liberty Zone (sec. 1400L)	Financing for the con-struction and rehabil-itation of nonreside-ntial real property and residential rental real	2002	No. Subject to a separate $8 billi-on issuance limitation.
22. Qualified green building and sustainable design projects (sec. 42(a)(14))	Projects designated by the Secretary, after consultation with the Environmental Protection Agency, as a green building and sustainable design project.	2004	No. Subject to a separate, national limitation of $2 billion of issuan-ce authority that may be allocated to eligible projects.

Table 4. (continued)

23. Qualified highway facilities (sec. 142(a)(15))	Any surface transport-tation or international bridge or tunnel proj-ect (for which an inte-rnational entity autho-rized under Federal or State law is response-ble) which receives Federal assis-tance under title 23 of the United States Code (relating to High-ways).	2005	No. Subject to a national limita-tion of $15 billi-on that the Secre-tary of Transpor-tation may allocate to qualified highway or surface freight transfer facilities.
24. Qualified surface freight transfer faci-lities (sec. 142(a)(16))	A facility for the transfer of freight from truck to rail or rail to truck which receives Federal assi-stance under title 23 or title 49 of the United States Code (relating to Transportation).	2005	No. Subject to a national limit-ation of $15 billion that the Secretary of Transportation may allocate to qualified high-way or surface freight transfer facilities.
25. Gulf Opportunity Zone (sec. 1400N)	Financing for the con-struction and rehabi-litation of residential and nonresidential property located in certain geographic areas of Mississippi, Louisiana, and Alabama affected by Hurricane Katrina.	2005	No. Subject to a separate limita-tion that is based on the population of the issuing State that resides within the Gulf Opportunity Zone.

Gulf tax Credit Bonds

Gulf tax credit bonds may be issued by the States of Louisiana, Mississippi, and Alabama. To qualify as Gulf tax credit bonds, 95 percent or more of the proceeds of such bonds must be used to (i) pay principal, interest, or premium on a bond (other than a private activity bond) that was outstanding on August 28, 2005, and was issued by the State issuing the Gulf tax credit bonds, or any political subdivision thereof, or (ii) make a loan to any political subdivision of such State to pay principal, interest, or premium on a bond issued by such political subdivision. In addition, the issuer of Gulf tax credit bonds must provide additional funds to pay principal, interest, or premium on outstanding bonds equal to the amount of Gulf tax credit bonds issued to repay such outstanding bonds. Gulf tax credit bonds must be a general obligation of the issuing State and must be designated by the Governor of such State. The maximum maturity on Gulf tax credit bonds is two years. The arbitrage rules restricting the ability of State and local governments to invest bond proceeds apply to Gulf tax credit bonds.

Table 5. Categories of Tax-Credit Bonds

Eligible Facility	Purpose	Code Authorized	Subject to General Private Activity Bond Volume Cap
1. Qualified zone academy bonds ("QZABs") (sec. 1397E)	Renovating, providing equipment to, developing course materials for use at, or training teachers and other school perso-nnel in certain public schools.	1997	Subject to an aggr-egate annual limi-tation of $400 million through 2005.
2. Clean renewable energy bonds ("CREBs") (sec. 54)	Financing of capital expenditures for facilities that qualify for the tax credit under section 45 for electricity production from renewable sources.	2005	Subject to an aggregate national limitation of $800 million.
3. Gulf tax credit bonds (sec. 1400N)	The payment of princ-ipal, interest, or premium on certain bonds issued by Mississippi, Louisi-ana, or Alabama.	2005	Subject to separate State limitations of $200 million in the case of Louisiana, $100 million in the case of Mississi-ppi, and $50 mill-ion in the case of Alabama.

Gulf tax credit bonds must be issued in calendar year 2006. The maximum amount of Gulf tax credit bonds that may be issued is $200 million in the case of Louisiana, $100 million in the case of Mississippi, and $50 million in the case of Alabama. Gulf tax credit bonds may not be used to pay principal, interest, or premium on any bond with respect to which there is any outstanding refunded or refunding bond. Gulf tax credit bonds may not be used to pay principal, interest, or premium on any prior bond if the proceeds of such prior bond were used to provide any of the following types of property: a private or commercial golf course, country club, massage parlor, hot tub facility, suntan facility, racetrack or other facility used for gambling, or any store the principal purpose of which is the sale of alcoholic beverages for consumption off premises.

As with CREBs, issuers of Gulf tax credit bonds are required to report issuance to the IRS in a manner similar to the information returns required for tax-exempt bonds.

End Notes

[1] This document may be cited as follows: Joint Committee on Taxation, *Present Law and Background Relating to State and Local Government Bonds* (JCX- 14-06), March 14, 2006.

[2] All section references are to the Internal Revenue Code of 1986 ("the Code") unless otherwise indicated.

[3] See Rev. Rul. 60-179, 1960-1 C.B. 37; Rev. Rul. 72-399, 1972-2 C.B. 73.

[4] For this purpose, the term "State" includes the District of Columbia and any possession of the United States (e.g., Puerto Rico, the U.S. Virgin Islands, Guam, American Samoa, and the Commonwealth of the Northern Mariana Islands).

[5] See *Commissioner v. Shamberg 's Estate, 144 F.2d 998 (2d Cir. 1944), cert. denied, 323 U.S. 792 (1945).*

[6] Sec. 150(d).

[7] Rev. Rul. 63-20, 1963-1 C.B. 24; Rev. Proc. 82-26, 1982-1 C.B. 476.

[8] Sec. 7871.

[9] Sec. 7871(c).

[10] For these purposes, the term "nongovernmental person" generally includes the Federal Government and all other individuals and entities other than States or local governments.

[11] Exempt facility bonds are bonds issued to finance: (1) airports; (2) docks and wharves; (3) mass commuting facilities; (4) high-speed intercity rail facilities; (5) facilities for the furnishing of water; (6) sewage facilities; (7) solid waste disposal facilities; (8) hazardous waste disposal facilities; (9) qualified residential rental projects; (10) facilities for the local furnishing of electric energy or gas; (11) local district heating or cooling facilities; (12) environmental enhancements of hydroelectric generating facilities; (13) qualified public educational facilities; (14) qualified green building and sustainable design projects; or (15) qualified highway or surface freight transfer facilities (sec. 142(a)).

[12] Sec. 141(e).

[13] Column 5 of Table 1, below, may be used to illustrate the measure of the subsidy measured as a percentage of the otherwise applicable taxable rate for the period 1986-2005.

[14] This may be represented as $r_e = (1-t)r$, where r_e is the tax-exempt yield, t is the investor's marginal tax rate, and r is the taxable bond yield.

[15] Secs. 1397E, 54, and 1400N(l), respectively.

[16] The "face amount" (or par value) represents the value of a bond at maturity as stated on the bond certificate.

[17] On the other hand, if tax-credit bonds are issued at discount, i.e., less than par value, the issuer incurs interest cost to the extent its debt service payments will exceed the amount of proceeds received from the sale of the bonds. This may occur because the rate on a prospective issue of tax-credit bonds is set lower than what investors are willing to accept to purchase the bonds at par value. To illustrate, assume the credit rate on tax-credit bonds with a face amount of $100 is set at five percent. If investors do not view the five percent credit rate as an acceptable return given the riskiness of the investment, they will purchase the bonds for something less than $100, e.g., $90. Because the credit is determined by

reference to the face amount of bonds ($100), the investor purchasing tax-credit bonds at a discount ($90) receives a higher yield than the stated credit rate. However, the issuer must repay the full face value of the bonds, $100 in this example, even though it received less than $100 in proceeds.

[18] This is true provided that the taxpayer faces tax liability of at least the amount of the credit. Without sufficient tax liability, the proposed tax credit arrangement would not be as advantageous. Presumably, only taxpayers who anticipate having sufficient tax liability to be offset by the proposed credit would hold these bonds.

[19] The Treasury Department issued proposed regulations on March 26, 2004 that would require issuers of QZABs to spend proceeds with due diligence. Prop. Reg. sec. 1.1 397E- 1(h), 69 Fed. Reg. 15747 (March 26, 2004).

[20] In fact, until the Supreme Court clarified the issue in a 1988 decision, some questioned whether the Constitution precluded Congress from imposing restrictions on tax-exempt bonds. The exemption for interest on tax-exempt bonds initially was viewed as constitutionally protected under the doctrine of intergovernmental immunities. See *Pollock v. Farmers Loan & Trust Co.*, 157 U.S. 429, *modified*, 158 U.S. 601 (1895) (holding earlier income tax unconstitutional for various reasons, including the taxation of municipal bond interest). In *South Carolina v. Baker*, 108 S.Ct. 1355 (1988), the Supreme Court rejected the argument that the tax exemption for State and local bonds is constitutionally protected. The Supreme Court's decision in *Baker* removed most constitutional constraints on congressional action to tax and restrict municipal finance.

[21] "Revenue bonds" are bonds payable solely from revenue derived from the property financed with bond proceeds. For example, bonds payable solely from tolls generated from the use of a road financed with such bonds would be revenue bonds. In contrast, "general obligation bonds" are bonds secured by the "full faith and credit" of the issuer, i.e., the issuing government makes an unconditional pledge to use its taxing powers to raise revenues to support debt service payments on the bonds.

[22] Rev. Rul. 54-106, 1954-1 C.B. 28.

[23] Pub. L. No. 90-364.

[24] H.R. Rep. No. 90-533, at 32 (1968).

[25] The original exempt activities were: (1) residential real property for family units capable of maintaining families on a nontransient basis; (2) sports facilities; (3) convention or trade show facilities; (4) airports, docks, wharves, mass commuting facilities, parking facilities, or storage or training facilities related to one of the above; (5) sewage or solid waste disposal facilities, or facilities for local furnishing of electric energy, gas, or water; and (6) air or water pollution control facilities.

[26] Joint Committee on Taxation, *Tax Reform Proposals: Tax Treatment of State and Local Government Bonds* (JCS-23-85), July 16, 1985.

[27] Title XI of the Omnibus Reconciliation Act of 1980, Pub. L. No. 96-499.

[28] Under the information reporting requirements, the term "private activity bond" included IDBs, student loan bonds, and bonds issued by charitable, educational, religious, and scientific organizations (described in section 501(c)(3)).

[29] The general small issue exception does not apply to bonds issued after December 31, 1986. However, as discussed below, certain private business manufacturing facilities (including certain directly related and ancillary facilities) and certain farm land and equipment may be financed with small issue bonds under present law.

[30] Joint Committee on Taxation, *General Explanation of the Deficit Reduction Act of 1984* (JCS-41-84), December 31, 1984.

[31] *Id.* at 930.

[32] Pub. L. No. 98-369.

[33] Congress was concerned with the issuance of tax-exempt bonds combined with Federal guarantees. This combination resulted in a double subsidy for certain activities and created bonds that were more attractive than United States Treasury securities (the interest on which

is taxable). The present-law prohibition on Federal guarantees, and exceptions thereto, is contained in section 149(b).

[34] Joint Committee on Taxation, *General Explanation of the Tax Reform of 1986* (JCS-10-87), May 4, 1987.

[35] These effects may be present under present law, as well. For example, as discussed below, tax-exempt small-issue bonds may be issued for certain manufacturing facilities subject to limitations on the total capital expenditures incurred with respect to such facilities within a three-year test period.

[36] Pub. L. No. 99-5 14.

[37] See Part IV, A, below, for a description of present-law requirements for governmental bonds.

[38] Before subsequent amendment, the list of exempt facilities consisted of bonds issued to finance: airports; docks and wharves; mass commuting facilities; facilities for the furnishing of water; sewage and solid waste disposal facilities; hazardous waste disposal facilities; and multifamily residential rental projects.

[39] The general requirements for each category of qualified private activity bond are discussed below.

[40] In 1987, these amounts were $75 and $250 million, respectively. The lower amounts were to coincide with the termination of the mortgage bond program, but were kept in place although the 1986 Act extended the mortgage bond program through 1988. The mortgage bond program subsequently was extended several times before being made permanent by the Omnibus Budget Reconciliation Act of 1992.

[41] The Taxpayer Relief Act of 1997 repealed the $150 million limit for bonds issued after August 5, 1997, to finance capital expenditures incurred after such date.

[42] Pub. L. No. 100-647.

[43] Sec. 142(a)(11) and sec. 142(i). A high-speed intercity rail facility is a facility providing rail transportation of passengers and their baggage that uses vehicles that are reasonably expected to operate at speeds in excess of 150 miles per hour between scheduled stops.

[44] Sec. 146(g)(4).

[45] Pub. L. No. 102-486.

[46] Pub. L. No. 105-34.

[47] A series of extensions authorized issuance through 2005.

[48] Pub. L. No. 107-147. The New York Liberty Zone consists of all business addresses located on or south of Canal Street, East Broadway (east of its intersection with Canal Street), or Grand Street (east of its intersection with East Broadway) in the Borough of Manhattan.

[49] Pub. L. No. 108-357.

[50] Pub. L. No. 109-59.

[51] Pub. L. No. 109-58.

[52] Pub. L. No. 109-135.

[53] The "Gulf Opportunity Zone" is defined as that portion of the Hurricane Katrina Disaster Area determined by the President to warrant individual or individual and public assistance from the Federal Government under the Robert T. Stafford Disaster Relief and Emergency Assistance Act by reason of Hurricane Katrina.

[54] Pub. L. No. 105-277.

[55] Pub. L. No. 106-554.

[56] Although the volume cap is now indexed for inflation, as discussed above, a number of activities (e.g., qualified public education facilities, green bonds, highway and surface freight transfer facility bonds, New York Liberty Zone Bonds, Gulf Opportunity Zone Bonds) are not subject to the volume cap.

[57] As discussed in Part IV, B, below, unused volume cap generally may be carried forward for three years.

[58] S. Rep. No. 99-3 13, at 826 (1986).

[59] H.R. Rep. No. 99-426, at 514 (1985); S. Rep. No. 99-313, at 825-826 (1986)

[60] The original House bill that led to the 1986 Act would have repealed the ten-percent security or payment test, leaving only the ten-percent private business use test. H.R. Rep. No. 99-426, at 520 (1985).
[61] Pub. L. No. 99-5 14 (1986).
[62] This may be accomplished by securing the repayment of the bonds with generally applicable taxes, which, under Treas. Reg. Sec. 1.141-4(e), are not taken into account for purposes of the private security or payment test.
[63] There also is no loan to a private person in these transactions that would meet the private loan financing test.
[64] See Figure 1, page 25, for a comparison of the annual issuance volume of long-term governmental bonds and long-term qualified private activity bonds for 1993-2003.
[65] Sec. 57(a)(5).
[66] Sec. 146.
[67] Table 4, below, provides a list of privately-used facilities or property eligible for tax-exempt financing and applicable volume limitations.
[68] Local governments also lose control when tax-credit bond issuance authority is allocated at the Federal level (e.g., CREBs).
[69] Table 5, page 47, provides a list of facilities or property eligible for tax-credit bond financing and applicable volume limitations.
[70] The Treasury Department issued proposed regulations on March 26, 2004, that would require issuers of QZABs to spend proceeds with due diligence. Prop. Reg. sec. 1.1 397E-1(h), 69 Fed. Reg. 15747 (March 26, 2004).
[71] Sec. 141.
[72] The 10 percent private business test is reduced to five percent in the case of private business uses (and payments with respect to such uses) that are unrelated to any governmental use being financed by the issue.
[73] Treas. Reg. sec. 1.141-3(b)(4).
[74] Treas. Reg. sec. 1.141-4(c)(3).
[75] Table 4, page 41, provides a list of privately-used facilities or property eligible for tax-exempt financing and applicable volume limitations.
[76] Sec. 57(a)(5). Special rules apply to exclude refundings of bonds issued before August 8, 1986, and certain bonds issued before September 1, 1986.
[77] Sec. 142(a).
[78] The qualified mortgage bond rules are modified for certain residences located in areas affected by Hurricanes Katrina, Rita, and Wilma.
[79] Sec. 144(b)(1).
[80] Sec. 144(a)(4)(G) as added by sec. 340(a) of the American Jobs Creation Act of 2004, Pub. L. No. 108-357 (2004).
[81] The "Gulf Opportunity Zone" is defined as that portion of the Hurricane Katrina Disaster Area determined by the President to warrant individual or individual and public assistance from the Federal Government under the Robert T. Stafford Disaster Relief and Emergency Assistance Act by reason of Hurricane Katrina.
[82] The Omnibus Budget Reconciliation Act of 1993 authorized the designation of a total of nine empowerment zones and 95 enterprise communities to provide tax incentives for businesses to locate within certain geographic areas designated by the Secretaries of Housing and Urban Development ("HUD") and Agriculture.
[83] Sec. 1394(b).
[84] Sec. 1397C.
[85] Sec. 146.
[86] Sec. 146(f)(5).
[87] Sec. 147(b).
[88] Sec. 147(h).
[89] Treas. Reg. sec. 5f.103-2(g)(3).

[90] Secs. 103(a) and (b)(2).

[91] Sec. 149(d)(5).

[92] Sec. 149(d)(3). Bonds issued before 1986 and pursuant to certain transition rules contained in the Tax Reform Act of 1986 may be advance refunded more than one time in certain cases.

[93] Sec. 149(d)(2). Special rules apply for certain advance refundings in the New York Liberty Zone and the Gulf Opportunity Zone.

[94] The exceptions include guarantees by: the Federal Housing Administration, the Department of Veterans' Affairs, the Federal National Mortgage Association, the Federal Home Loan Mortgage Association, the Government National Mortgage Association; the Student Loan Marketing Association; and the Bonneville Power Authority pursuant to the Northwest Power Act (16 U.S.C. sec. 839d). The exception also includes guarantees for certain housing programs. These are: (a) private activity bonds for a qualified residential rental project or a housing program obligation under section 11(b) of the United States Housing Act of 1937; (b) a qualified mortgage bond; or (c) a qualified veterans' mortgage bond.

[95] Sec. 149(e).

[96] Secs. 1397E, 54, and 1400N(l), respectively.

In: Role of Tax Preferences in Financial… ISBN: 978-1-61668-546-1
Editors: Michael D. Scott

Chapter 2

PRESENT LAW AND ISSUES RELATED TO INFRASTRUCTURE FINANCE

Joint Committee on Taxation

INTRODUCTION AND SUMMARY

The Committee on Ways and Means has scheduled a public hearing on October 29, 2008 on economic recovery, job creation and investment in America. Among the issues the Committee will consider is the ability of State and local governments to finance infrastructure needs. This document[1] provides a description of present law relating to tax-exempt bonds issued by State and local governments and a description of present law relating to tax-credit bonds, both of which operate to deliver a Federal subsidy to eligible borrowers, albeit by different mechanisms and with different degrees of efficiency. The document also provides background data and an economic discussion of tax-exempt bonds and tax-credit bonds.

Tax-Exempt Bonds

Interest paid on bonds issued by State and local governments generally is excluded from gross income for Federal income tax purposes. Because the income is excludible, investors generally are willing to accept a lower rate of interest on tax-exempt bonds than they might otherwise accept on a taxable investment. This, in turn, lowers the borrowing cost for the beneficiaries of such financing.

Bonds issued by State and local governments may be classified as either governmental bonds or private activity bonds. Governmental bonds are bonds the proceeds of which are primarily used to finance governmental functions or which are repaid with governmental funds. Private activity bonds are bonds in which the State or local government serves as a conduit providing financing to nongovernmental persons (e.g., private businesses or individuals). The exclusion from income for State and local bonds does not apply to private activity bonds unless the bonds are issued for certain permitted purposes ("qualified private activity bonds") and other Code requirements are met.

Like other activities carried out and paid for by State and local governments, the construction, renovation, and operation of governmental transportation infrastructure projects such as public highways or governmental mass commuting systems (e.g., rail and bus) are eligible for financing with the proceeds of governmental bonds. In addition, certain privately owned and/or operated infrastructure projects may be financed with qualified private activity bonds.

Tax-Credit Bonds

Tax-credit bonds are not interest-bearing obligations. Rather, the taxpayer holding a tax-credit bond on a credit allowance date is entitled to a tax credit in lieu of an interest payment. In the Code, there are currently tax-credit bonds for qualified zone academies ("QZABs"), tax-credit bonds for capital expenditures relating to certain renewable energy facilities (clean renewable energy bonds "CREBs" and "New CREBs"), Gulf tax-credit bonds, Midwest tax- credit bonds, qualified energy conservation bonds, and qualified forestry conservation bonds.

Economic Discussion of Tax-Exempt Bonds and Tax-Credit Bonds

Tax-exempt financing provides an implicit Federal subsidy to the borrower (i.e., either the qualified governmental unit or the conduit borrower) but, in practice, some of the subsidy also redounds to the bond investor (the lender). Because interest income on the bonds is excluded from gross income, the bond investor is willing to accept a lower interest rate on the bonds than he might otherwise accept on an identical taxable investment. Thus, the borrower receives an implicit Federal subsidy equal to the difference between the tax-exempt interest rate paid and the taxable rate that otherwise would be paid. In this way, the income exclusion lowers the cost of capital for the State and local governments (or private parties in the case of private activity bonds). The bond investor also receives a Federal subsidy from tax-exempt financing equal to the difference between the tax-exempt interest rate and the after-tax yield on a taxable investment. The bond investor's willingness to purchase tax-exempt bonds also depends on the bond investor's marginal tax rate. The fact that some bond investors receive a tax benefit greater than the reduction in interest cost achieved by the borrower is a source of economic inefficiency in tax-exempt bonds.

Under present law, the subsidy provided by tax-credit bonds is deeper than the subsidy for tax-exempt bonds. This is because (if the bonds are not issued at discount) the issuer of tax- credit bonds pays no interest, only principal. The "interest" is paid by the Federal Government in the form of tax credits. The credit is includible in gross income of the bond investor as if it were an interest payment on the bond, and can be claimed against regular income tax liability and alternative minimum tax liability. With a tax-credit bond, the bond investor's tax saving is independent of his or her marginal tax rate. As a consequence, with a tax-credit bond, the loss in Federal receipts from the tax credit equals the reduction in the tax-credit bond issuer's interest cost.

For most present-law categories of tax-credit bonds, the credit rate on the bonds is determined by the Secretary of the Treasury and is an estimate of the rate that permits issuance of such bonds without discount and interest cost to the qualified issuer. That is, the tax credit generally is chosen to approximate an interest rate subsidy of 100 percent. In the case of new CREBs and qualified energy conservation bonds the tax credit rate is chosen to equal 70 percent of the credit rate that would be provided to the other present-law tax credit bonds.

I. Tax-Exempt Bonds

A. Overview

Interest paid on bonds issued by State and local governments generally is excluded from gross income for Federal income tax purposes.[2] Because the income is excludible, investors generally are willing to accept a lower rate of interest on tax-exempt bonds than they might otherwise accept on a taxable investment. This, in turn, lowers the borrowing cost for the beneficiaries of such financing.

Bonds issued by State and local governments may be classified as either governmental bonds or private activity bonds. Governmental bonds are bonds the proceeds of which are primarily used to finance governmental functions or which are repaid with governmental funds. Private activity bonds are bonds in which the State or local government serves as a conduit providing financing to nongovernmental persons (e.g., private businesses or individuals). The exclusion from income for State and local bonds does not apply to private activity bonds, unless the bonds are issued for certain permitted purposes ("qualified private activity bonds") and other Code requirements are met.

Like other activities carried out and paid for by State and local governments, the construction, renovation, and operation of governmental transportation infrastructure projects such as public highways or governmental mass commuting systems (e.g., rail and bus) are eligible for financing with the proceeds of governmental bonds. In addition, certain privately owned and/or operated infrastructure projects may be financed with qualified private activity bonds.

B. Tax-Exempt Governmental Bonds and Private Activity Bonds

In General

Present law does not limit the types of facilities that can be financed with governmental bonds. Thus, State and local governments can issue tax-exempt, governmental bonds to finance a broad range of transportation infrastructure projects, including highways, railways, airports, etc. However, while the types of projects eligible for governmental bond financing are not circumscribed, present law imposes restrictions on the parties that may benefit from such financing. For example, present law limits the amount of governmental bond proceeds that can be used by nongovernmental persons. Use of bond proceeds by nongovernmental persons in excess of amounts permitted by present law may result in such bonds being treated as taxable private activity bonds, rather than tax-exempt governmental bonds. The Code[3] does not expressly define a "governmental bond." Instead it defines a private activity bond as any bond that satisfies (1) the private business use test and the private security or payment test ("the private business test"); or (2) "the private loan financing test."[4] Generally, private activity bonds are taxable unless issued as qualified private activity bonds.

Generally, governmental bonds are not subject to restrictions that apply to bonds used to finance private activities. For example, governmental bonds are not subject to issuance cost, maturity, and annual volume limitations that generally apply to qualified private activity bonds.

Private Business Test

Under the private business test, a bond is a private activity bond if it is part of an issue in which:

1. More than 10 percent of the proceeds of the issue (including use of the bond-financed property) are to be used in the trade or business of any person other than a governmental unit ("private business use"); and
2. More than 10 percent of the payment of principal or interest on the issue is, directly or indirectly, secured by (a) property used or to be used for a private business use or (b) to be derived from payments in respect of property, or borrowed money, used or to be used for a private business use ("private payment test").[5]

A bond is not a private activity bond unless both parts of the private business test (i.e., the private business use test and the private payment test) are met. Thus, a facility that is 100 percent privately used does not cause the bonds financing such facility to be private activity bonds if the bonds are not secured by or paid with private payments. For example, land improvements that benefit a privately-owned factory may be financed with governmental bonds if the debt service on such bonds is not paid by the factory owner or other private parties.

A contract between a private management or other service company and a governmental unit to operate bond-financed governmental facilities may result in private business use depending on the terms of the contract.[6] In general, a management contract gives rise to private business use if the compensation under the contract is based on net profits. For example, a management contract with respect to a commuter rail facility that compensates the management company based on the profits of such facility would result in private use. Contracts for service incidental to the facility's primary functions, such as janitorial, office equipment repair and similar services, are not considered management contracts.

For purposes of the private payment test, both direct and indirect payments made by any private person treated as using the financed property are taken into account. Payments by a person for the use of proceeds generally do not include payments for ordinary and necessary expenses (within the meaning of section 162) attributable to the operation and maintenance of financed property.[7]

Private Loan Financing Test

A bond issue satisfies the private loan financing test if proceeds exceeding the lesser of $5 million or five percent of such proceeds are used directly or indirectly to finance loans to one or more nongovernmental persons. Private loans include both business and other (e.g., personal) uses and payments by private persons; however, in the case of business uses and payments, all private loans also constitute private business uses and payments subject to the private business test.

C. Qualified Private Activity Bonds

In General

Qualified private activity bonds are tax-exempt bonds issued to provide financing for specified privately used facilities. The definition of a qualified private activity bond includes an exempt facility bond, or qualified mortgage, veterans' mortgage, small issue, redevelopment, 501(c)(3), or student loan bond.[8]

Exempt Facility Bonds for Infrastructure

To qualify as an exempt facility bond, 95 percent of the net proceeds must be used to finance an eligible facility.[9] Business facilities eligible for this financing include transportation (airports, ports, local mass commuting, high-speed intercity rail facilities, and qualified highway or surface freight transfer facilities) and privately owned and/or operated public works facilities.

Airports

Exempt facility bonds may be issued to finance airports. Exempt facility bonds for airports are not subject to the State volume cap. However, all tax-exempt-bond-financed airport property must be governmentally owned. Property eligible for this financing includes land, terminals, runways, public parking facilities, and related equipment. Airplanes are not eligible for tax-exempt financing. Additionally, certain real property facilities (and related equipment) are excluded from this financing.

Port Facilities

Exempt-facility bonds may be issued to finance port ("dock and wharf") facilities and related storage and training facilities. Facilities that are specifically ineligible for financing with airport bonds may not be financed with port bonds. Further, ships and other vessels are not eligible for private activity tax-exempt bond financing. All property financed with these bonds must be governmentally owned. Exempt facility bonds issued for ports are not subject to the State volume cap described below.

Mass Commuting Facilities

Exempt facility bond financing for mass commuting facilities is subject to similar restrictions as those which apply to such bonds for airports and ports. All property financed with these bonds must be governmentally owned. Further, "rolling stock" (e.g., buses and rail cars) are not eligible for financing with exempt facility bonds.

High-Speed Intercity Rail Facilities

The definition of an exempt facility bond includes bonds issued to finance high-speed intercity rail facilities.[10] A facility qualifies as a high-speed intercity rail facility if it is a facility (other than rolling stock) for fixed guideway rail transportation of passengers and their baggage between metropolitan statistical areas.[11] The facilities must use vehicles that are reasonably expected to operate at speeds in excess of 150 miles per hour between scheduled stops, and the facilities must be made available to members of the general public as passengers.

Unlike other bond-financed transportation facilities, high-speed intercity rail facilities may be privately owned. However, if the bonds are to be issued for a nongovernmental owner of the facility, such owner must irrevocably elect not to claim depreciation or credits with respect to the property financed by the net proceeds of the issue.[12]

The Code imposes a special redemption requirement for these types of bonds. Any proceeds not used within three years of the date of issuance of the bonds must be used within the following six months to redeem such bonds.[13]

Seventy-five percent of the principal amount of the bonds issued for high-speed rail facilities is exempt from the volume limit.[14] If all the property to be financed by the net proceeds of the issue is to be owned by a governmental unit, then such bonds are completely exempt from the volume limit.

Qualified Highway or Surface Freight Transfer Facility Bonds

Present law authorizes the issuance pf tax-exempt private activity bonds to finance qualified highway or surface freight transfer facilities. A qualified highway facility or surface freight transfer facility is any surface transportation or international bridge or tunnel project (for which an international entity authorized under Federal or State law is responsible) which receives Federal assistance under title 23 of the United States Code or any facility for the transfer of freight from truck to rail or rail to truck which receives Federal assistance under title 23 or title 49 of the United States Code.

Qualified highway or surface freight transfer facility bonds are not subject to the State volume limitations. Rather, the Secretary of Transportation is authorized to allocate a total of $15 billion of issuance authority to qualified highway or surface freight transfer facilities in such manner as the Secretary determines appropriate.[15]

Similar to the requirement for high-speed intercity rail facilities, the Code imposes a special redemption requirement for qualified highway or surface freight transfer facility bonds. Under present law, the proceeds of qualified highway or surface freight transfer facility bonds must be spent on qualified projects within five years from the date of issuance of such bonds. Proceeds that remain unspent after five years must be used to redeem outstanding bonds.

Sewage Facilities

The Code permits the issuance of exempt facility bonds for sewage facilities. This includes property used for certain levels of treatment of wastewater and property used for collection, storage, use, processing, or final disposal of wastewater, sewage, septage.

Water Facilities

The Code permits the issuance of exempt facility bonds for water facilities. This provision covers facilities furnishing water that is made available to the general public, including electric utility, industrial, agricultural, or other commercial users. Such facilities must be operated by a governmental unit or the rates for sale of water must be approved by a governmental unit.

Facilities for the Local Furnishing of Electric Energy or Gas

The Code permits the issuance of exempt facility bonds for facilities for the local furnishing of electric energy or gas. This generally includes a facility furnishing electric energy or gas serving an area not to exceed two contiguous counties or a city and one contiguous county.

Local District Heating or Cooling Facilities

The Code permits the issuance of exempt facility bonds for local district heating and cooling facilities. Such a facility provides hot water, chilled water, or steam to two or more users for residential, commercial, or industrial heating or cooling, or process steam.

Hazardous Waste Disposal Facilities

Facilities for the incineration or permanent entombment of hazardous waste are permitted to be financed by exempt facility bonds if certain requirements are met.

Other Qualified Private Activity Bonds

Other Exempt Facility Bonds

In addition to exempt facility bonds for transportation and privately owned and/or operated public works facilities discussed above, tax-exempt exempt facility bonds may be used for privately-owned and/or operated residential rental housing, qualified public educational facilities, and qualified green building and sustainable design projects. Environmental enhancements of hydro-electric generating facilities also may qualify for exempt facility bonds.

Qualified Mortgage Bonds

Owner-occupied housing may be financed with qualified mortgage bonds. Qualified mortgage bonds are bonds issued to make mortgage loans to qualified mortgagors for the purchase, improvement, or rehabilitation of owner-occupied residences. The Code imposes several limitations on qualified mortgage bonds, including income limitations for homebuyers and purchase price limitations for the home financed with bond proceeds. In addition to these limitations, qualified mortgage bonds generally cannot be used to finance a mortgage for a homebuyer who had an ownership interest in a principal residence in the three years preceding the execution of the mortgage (the "first-time homebuyer" requirement). Special income and purchase price limitations and first-time homebuyer waivers apply to targeted area residences and in certain disaster areas. Also, the Code provides an exception from the first-time homebuyer requirement for certain veterans provided that the veteran has not previously received financing under any State's qualified mortgage bond program.

Qualified mortgage bonds also may be used to finance qualified home-improvement loans. Qualified home-improvement loans are defined as loans to finance alterations, repairs, and improvements on an existing residence, but only if such alterations, repairs, and improvements substantially protect or improve the basic livability or energy efficiency of the property. Generally, qualified home-improvement loans may not exceed $15,000, however special rules apply for certain disaster areas, including increasing the loan maximum.

Qualified Veterans' Mortgage Bonds

Qualified veterans' mortgage bonds are bonds the proceeds of which are used to finance the purchase, or qualifying rehabilitation or improvement, of single-family, owner-occupied residences of qualified veterans located within the jurisdiction of the issuer of the bonds. A qualified veterans' mortgage bond may be issued only by those States that issued such bonds before June 22, 1984. These States are Alaska, California, Oregon, Texas, and Wisconsin. Annual issuance of qualified veterans' mortgage bonds is subject to a separate State limit, but not to the unified State volume cap applicable to most other private activity bonds.

Persons receiving qualified veterans' mortgage bond loans must be veterans who served on active duty, and who applied for the financing before the date 25 years after the last date on which the borrower left active service. There are no restrictions on purchase price or borrower income, and no first-time homebuyer requirement for qualified veterans' mortgage bond loans.

Student Loan Bonds

Qualified student loan bonds are bonds issued to finance eligible student loans. Interest on qualified student loan bonds is tax-exempt. Eligible student loans include Federally guaranteed loans under the Higher Education Act of 1965 and other loans financed as part of a program of general application approved by the State.[16]

Small Issue Bonds

Qualified small issue bonds are tax-exempt bonds issued by State and local governments to finance private business manufacturing facilities (including certain directly related and ancillary facilities) or the acquisition of land and equipment by certain farmers. In both instances, these bonds are subject to limits on the amount of financing that may be provided, both for a single borrowing and in the aggregate.

Redevelopment Bonds

Qualified redevelopment bonds are bonds issued as part of an issue 95-percent or more of the net proceeds of which is to be used for one or more redevelopment purposes in a designated "blighted area." A blighted area is an area designated as such by the local governing body of such area based on the substantial presence of factors such as excessive vacant, abandoned or vacant buildings, substandard structures, vacancies, and delinquencies in payment of real property taxes.

Qualified 501(c)(3) Bonds

State and local governments may issue tax-exempt bonds to finance the activities of charitable organizations described in section 501(c)(3) ("qualified 501 (c)(3) bonds"). The beneficiaries of this type of financing frequently are private, nonprofit hospitals and private, nonprofit colleges and universities. Both capital expenditures and limited working capital expenditures of charitable organizations described in section 501 (c)(3) of the Code may be financed with qualified 501(c)(3) bonds.

Qualified 501(c)(3) bonds are not subject to the State volume cap.

New York Liberty Zone Bonds

Present law permits an aggregate of $8 billion in exempt facility bonds for the purpose of financing the construction and rehabilitation of nonresidential real property and residential rental real property in a designated "Liberty

Zone" of New York City ("Liberty Zone Bonds"). Liberty Zone Bonds must be issued before January 1, 2010, and are not subject to the State volume cap.

Gulf Opportunity Zone Bonds

Present law permits the issuance of qualified private activity bonds to finance the construction and rehabilitation of residential and nonresidential property located in the Gulf Opportunity Zone ("Gulf Opportunity Zone Bonds").[17] Gulf Opportunity Zone Bonds must be issued before January 1, 2011.

Midwestern Disaster Area Bonds

Present law provides tax-exempt bond financing like Gulf Opportunity Zone Bonds with certain modifications to the Midwestern disaster area.[18] Specifically, it allows the issuance of qualified private activity bonds ("qualified Midwestern disaster area bonds") to finance the construction and rehabilitation of certain residential and nonresidential property located in the Midwestern disaster area. Qualified Midwestern disaster area bonds must be issued before January 1, 2013. Other tax-exempt bond rules that apply to Gulf Opportunity Zone Bonds generally apply to qualified Midwestern disaster area bonds.

Hurricane Ike Disaster Area Bonds

Present law provides tax-exempt bond financing like Gulf Opportunity Zone Bonds with certain modifications to Louisiana, and Texas, (or any political subdivisions thereof). Specifically, it allows the issuance of qualified private activity bonds ("Hurricane Ike disaster area bonds") to finance the construction and rehabilitation of certain residential and nonresidential property located in the Hurricane Ike disaster area.[19] Hurricane Ike disaster area bonds must be issued before January 1, 2013. Other tax-exempt bond rules that apply to Gulf Opportunity Zone Bonds generally apply to Hurricane Ike disaster bonds.

Tax-Exempt Enterprise Zone Facility Bonds

Enterprise zone facility bonds are issued to finance "enterprise zone facilities" located in "enterprise communities" or "empowerment zones" if the principal users of such facilities are "qualified enterprise zone businesses." Ninety-five percent or more of the net proceeds of the bonds must be used to provide an enterprise zone facility. An enterprise zone facility is defined as any qualified zone property the principal user of which is an "enterprise zone business," and any land that is functionally related and subordinate to such property.[20] Enterprise zone businesses are defined as certain partnerships or corporations conducting a qualified business in, and employing residents of, an empowerment zone.[21]

Additional Qualified Private Activity Bonds Requirements

Volume Cap

Unlike governmental bonds, the aggregate volume of most qualified private activity bonds is restricted by the annual volume cap imposed on issuers within each State.[22] As discussed above, the volume cap rules reflect Congress' intent to control the total volume of tax- exempt bonds issued for private activities. For calendar year 2008, the State volume cap, which is indexed for inflation, equals $85 per resident of the State, or $262.09 million, if greater.

Exceptions from the volume cap are provided for bonds for certain governmentally owned facilities (e.g., airports, ports, high-speed intercity rail, and solid waste disposal) and bonds issued to finance the activities of certain charitable organizations. In addition, bonds which are subject to separate local, State, or national volume limits are not subject to the unified volume cap (e.g., public/private educational facility bonds, enterprise zone facility bonds, qualified green building bonds, and qualified highway or surface freight transfer facility bonds).

If an issuer's volume cap for a calendar year exceeds the aggregate amount of tax-exempt private activity bonds issued during the year, the authority may elect to treat all (or any portion) of the excess as a carryforward for one or more specified "carryforward purposes." The issuing authority is required to identify the purpose for which the carryforward is elected and specify the portion of the carryforward which is to be used for that purpose. The Code defines "carryforward purpose" to mean one of four purposes: issuing exempt facility bonds; issuing qualified mortgage bonds or mortgage credit certificates; issuing qualified student loan bonds; and issuing qualified redevelopment bonds.[23] Carryforwards of unused volume cap are valid for three years.

Maturity Limitations

Most qualified private activity bonds are subject to a term to maturity rule which limits the period of time such bonds may remain outstanding.

Generally, this rule provides that the average maturity of a qualified private activity bond cannot exceed 120 percent of the economic life of the property being financed.[24] The term to maturity rule does not apply to qualified mortgage or student loan bonds.[25]

Issuance Costs

Generally, the amount of costs of issuance (e.g., bond counsel and underwriter fees) that may be paid from qualified private activity bond proceeds is limited to two percent. In addition, amounts paid for costs of issuance are not treated as spent for the exempt purpose of the borrowing (i.e., are not "good costs").

Public Approval

To be a qualified private activity bond, a bond must satisfy a public approval requirement including providing reasonable public notice for a hearing. Regardless of State and local law, reasonable public notice must include notice "published in one or more newspapers of general circulation available to residents of that locality or if announced by radio or television broadcast to those residents."[26]

Prohibited Facilities

Qualified private activity bonds generally are subject to restrictions on the use of proceeds for the acquisition of land and existing property, use of proceeds to finance certain specified facilities (e.g., airplanes, skyboxes, other luxury boxes, health club facilities, gambling facilities, and liquor stores), and use of proceeds to pay costs of issuance. Small-issue and redevelopment bonds also are subject to additional restrictions on the use of proceeds for certain facilities (e.g., golf courses and massage parlors).

D. Rules Applicable to All Tax-Exempt Bonds

Arbitrage Restrictions

To prevent the issuance of Federally subsidized tax-exempt bonds that do not directly support governmental projects or specified activities, the tax exemption for State and local bonds does not apply to any arbitrage bond.[27] An arbitrage bond is defined as any bond that is part of an issue if any proceeds of the issue are reasonably expected to be used (or intentionally are used) to acquire higher yielding investments or to replace funds that are used to acquire higher yielding investments.[28] In general, arbitrage profits may be earned only during specified periods (e.g., defined "temporary periods") before funds are needed for the purpose of the borrowing or on specified types of investments (e.g., "reasonably required reserve or replacement funds"). Subject to limited exceptions, investment profits that are earned during these periods or on such investments must be rebated to the Federal government ("arbitrage rebate").

Advance Refundings

A refunding bond is defined as any bond used to pay principal, interest, or redemption price on a prior bond issue (the refunded bond). The Code contains different rules for "current" as opposed to advance refunding bonds. A current refunding occurs when the refunded bond is redeemed within 90 days of issuance of the refunding bonds. Conversely, a bond is classified as an advance refunding if it is issued more than 90 days before the redemption of the refunded bond (thus, two or more issues of tax-exempt bonds are outstanding simultaneously).[29] An advance refunding often takes place when interest rates fall and the issuer, in an effort to save money, seeks to redeem an existing issue with new funds borrowed at a lower rate. If the existing issue has "call protection," that is, provisions of the bonds that prohibit redemption by the issuer for a period of years in order to protect the holders, the issuer cannot immediately redeem the existing bond issue with the proceeds of the advance refunding bond issue. For that reason, proceeds of advance refunding bonds are generally invested in an escrow account and held until a future date when the refunded bond may be redeemed.

Although there is no statutory limitation on the number of times that tax-exempt bonds may be currently refunded, the Code limits advance refundings. Generally, governmental bonds and qualified 501(c)(3) bonds may be advance refunded one time.[30] Private activity bonds, other than qualified 501(c)(3) bonds, may not be advance refunded at all.[31]

Federal Guarantees

Generally, interest on State and local bonds that are Federally guaranteed does not qualify for tax exemption. A bond is Federally guaranteed if: (1) the payment of principal or interest with respect to such bond is guaranteed (in whole or in part) by the United States (or any agency or instrumentality thereof); (2) such bond is issued as part of an issue and five percent of more of the proceeds of such issue is to be (a) used in making loans the payment of principal or interest with respect to which is guaranteed (in whole or in part) by the United States (or any agency or instrumentality thereof), or (b) invested directly or indirectly in federally insured deposits or accounts; or (3) the payment of principal or interest on such bond is otherwise indirectly guaranteed (in whole or in part) by the United States (or any agency or instrumentality thereof).

The Federal guarantee restriction was enacted in 1984 with certain exceptions for certain guarantee programs in existence at that time.[32] In response to current market instability, the Department of the Treasury is making available certain funds from its Exchange Stabilization Fund on a temporary basis to certain money market funds to enable the funds to maintain stable $1.00 per share net asset values. Notice 2008-81 provides that the program will not result in any violations of the restrictions against Federal guarantees of tax-exempt bonds with respect to the tax-exempt bond assets of tax-exempt money market funds, as defined by the notice.

Information Returns

An issuer of bonds must file with the IRS certain information in order for the interest on such bond to be tax-exempt.[33] Generally, this information return is required to be filed no later the 15th day of the second month after the close of the calendar quarter in which the bonds were issued.

II. Tax-Credit Bonds

In General

Tax-credit bonds are not interest-bearing obligations. Rather, the taxpayer holding a tax- credit bond on a credit allowance date is entitled to a tax credit. In the Code, there are currently tax-credit bonds for qualified zone academies ("QZABs"), tax-credit bonds for capital expenditures relating to certain renewable energy facilities (clean renewable energy bonds, "CREBs" and "New CREBs"), Gulf Tax-credit Bonds, Midwest Tax-credit Bonds, qualified energy conservation bonds, and qualified forestry conservation bonds.

Types of Tax-Credit Bonds

Qualified Zone Academy Bonds

QZABs are defined as any bond issued by a State or local government, provided that (1) at least 95 percent of the proceeds are used for the purpose of renovating, providing equipment to, developing course materials for use at, or training teachers and other school personnel in a "qualified zone academy," and (2) private entities have promised to contribute to the qualified zone academy certain equipment, technical assistance or training, employee services, or other property or services with a value equal to at least 10 percent of the bond proceeds.

A school is a "qualified zone academy" if (1) the school is a public school that provides education and training below the college level, (2) the school operates a special academic program in cooperation with businesses to enhance the academic curriculum and increase graduation and employment rates, and (3) either (a) the school is located in an empowerment zone or enterprise community designated under the Code, or (b) it is reasonably expected that at least 35 percent of the students at the school will be eligible for free or reduced-cost lunches under the school lunch program established under the National School Lunch Act.

A total of $400 million of QZABs has been authorized to be issued annually in calendar years 1998 through 2009. The $400 million aggregate bond cap is allocated to the States according to their respective populations of individuals below the poverty line. Each State, in turn, allocates the credit authority to qualified zone academies within such State.

Gulf Tax-Credit Bonds and Midwest Tax-Credit Bonds

Gulf tax-credit bonds may be issued by the States of Louisiana, Mississippi, and Alabama. To qualify as Gulf tax-credit bonds, 95 percent or more of the proceeds of such bonds must be used to (i) pay principal, interest, or premium on a bond (other than a private activity bond) that was outstanding on August 28, 2005, and was issued by the State issuing the Gulf tax- credit bonds, or any political subdivision thereof, or (ii) make a loan to any political subdivision of such State to pay principal, interest, or premium on a bond issued by such political subdivision. In addition, the issuer of Gulf tax-credit bonds must provide additional funds to pay principal, interest, or premium on outstanding bonds equal to the amount of Gulf tax-credit bonds issued to repay such outstanding bonds. Gulf tax-credit bonds must be a general obligation of the issuing State and must be designated by the Governor of such State. The maximum maturity on Gulf tax-credit bonds is two years. The arbitrage rules restricting the ability of State and local governments to invest bond proceeds apply to Gulf tax-credit bonds.

Gulf tax-credit bonds must be issued in calendar year 2006. The maximum amount of Gulf tax-credit bonds that may be issued is $200 million in the case of Louisiana, $100 million in the case of Mississippi, and $50 million in the case of Alabama. Gulf tax-credit bonds may not be used to pay principal, interest, or premium on any bond with respect to which there is any outstanding refunded or refunding bond. Gulf tax-credit bonds may not be used to pay principal, interest, or premium on any prior bond if the proceeds of such prior bond were used to provide any of the following types of property: a private or commercial golf course, country club, massage parlor, hot tub facility, suntan facility, racetrack or other facility used for gambling, or any store the principal purpose of which is the sale of alcoholic beverages for consumption off premises.

Also, present law allows Midwestern tax-credit bonds to be issued in 2009 by any State in which a Midwestern disaster area is located (or any instrumentality of the State). The operation and effect of these Midwestern tax-credit bonds are otherwise identical to Gulf tax-credit bonds except for different volume caps. Under the provision, the maximum amount of Midwestern tax-credit bonds that may be issued is: (1) $100 million for any State with an aggregate population located in all Midwestern disaster areas within the State of at least 2,000,000; (2) (1) $50 million for any State with an aggregate population located in all Midwestern disaster areas within the State of at least 1,000,000 but less than 2,000,000; and (3) $0 for any other State. This provision is effective for bonds issued after December 31, 2008.

Qualified Energy Conservation Bonds

The Energy Improvement and Extension Act of 2008 created a new category of tax-credit bonds, qualified energy conservation bonds. Qualified energy conservation bonds may be used to finance qualified conservation purposes.

The term "qualified conservation purpose" means:

1. Capital expenditures incurred for purposes of reducing energy consumption in publicly owned buildings by at least 20 percent; implementing green community programs; rural development involving the production of electricity from renewable energy

resources; or any facility eligible for the production tax credit under section 45 (other than Indian coal and refined coal production facilities);

2. Expenditures with respect to facilities or grants that support research in: (A) development of cellulosic ethanol or other nonfossil fuels; (B) technologies for the capture and sequestration of carbon dioxide produced through the use of fossil fuels; (C) increasing the efficiency of existing technologies for producing nonfossil fuels; (D) automobile battery technologies and other technologies to reduce fossil fuel consumption in transportation; and (E) technologies to reduce energy use in buildings;
3. Mass commuting facilities and related facilities that reduce the consumption of energy, including expenditures to reduce pollution from vehicles used for mass commuting;
4. Demonstration projects designed to promote the commercialization of: (A) green building technology; (B) conversion of agricultural waste for use in the production of fuel or otherwise; (C) advanced battery manufacturing technologies; (D) technologies to reduce peak-use of electricity; and (D) technologies for the capture and sequestration of carbon dioxide emitted from combusting fossil fuels in order to produce electricity; and
5. Public education campaigns to promote energy efficiency (other than movies, concerts, and other events held primarily for entertainment purposes).

There is a national limitation on qualified energy conservation bonds of $800 million. The credit rate for qualified energy conservation bonds is set by the Secretary at a rate that is 70 percent (rather than 100 percent) of the rate that would permit issuance of such bonds without discount and interest cost to the issuer. Allocations of qualified energy conservation bonds are made to the States with sub-allocations to large local governments.

Clean Renewable Energy Bonds and New Clean Renewable Energy Bonds

CREBs and New CREBs are used to finance capital expenditures incurred by qualified borrowers for facilities that qualify for the tax credit under section 45 (other than Indian coal production facilities and, in the case of New CREBs, refined coal facilities), without regard to the placed-in-service date requirements of that section. There is a national CREB limitation of $1.2

million. Of that amount, no more than $750 million may be allocated to governmental bodies. CREBs must be issued before December 31, 2009.

For New CREBs, there is a national limitation of $800 million. Unlike CREBs, however, the credit rate on New CREBs is set by the Secretary at a rate that is 70 percent (rather than 100 percent) of the rate that would permit issuance of such bonds without discount and interest cost to the issuer. No more than one-third of the national limit may be allocated to projects of public power providers, governmental bodies, or cooperative electric companies. Allocations to governmental bodies and cooperative electric companies may be made in the manner the Secretary determines appropriate. Allocations to projects of public power providers are to be made, to the extent practicable, in such manner that the amount allocated to each such project bears the same ratio to the cost of such project as the maximum allocation limitation to projects of public power providers bears to the cost of all such projects.

Qualified Forestry Conservation Bonds

Qualified forestry conservation bonds are bonds issued by qualified issuers to finance qualified forestry conservation projects. The term "qualified issuer" means a State or a section 501 (c)(3) organization. The term "qualified forestry conservation project" means the acquisition by a State or section 501(c)(3) organization from an unrelated person of forest and forest land that meets the following qualifications: (1) some portion of the land acquired must be adjacent to United States Forest Service Land; (2) at least half of the land acquired must be transferred to the United States Forest Service at no net cost and not more than half of the land acquired may either remain with or be donated to a State; (3) all of the land must be subject to a habitat conservation plan for native fish approved by the United States Fish and Wildlife Service; and (4) the amount of acreage acquired must be at least 40,000 acres.

A qualified issuer receiving an allocation to issue qualified forestry conservation bonds may, in lieu of issuing bonds, elect to treat such allocation as a deemed payment of tax (regardless of whether the issuer is subject to tax under chapter 1 of the Code) that is equal to 50 percent of the amount of such allocation. An election to treat an allocation of qualified forestry conservation bonds as a deemed payment is not valid unless the qualified issuer certifies to the Secretary that any payment of tax refunded to the issuer will be used exclusively for one or more qualified forestry conservation purposes. The deemed tax payment may not be used as an offset or credit against any other tax and shall not accrue interest. In addition, if the qualified issuer fails to use any portion of the overpayment for qualified forestry conservation purposes, the issuer shall be liable to the United States in an amount equal to such portion, plus interest, for the period from the date such portion was refunded to the date such amount is paid.

General Rules Applicable to Qualified Tax-Credit Bonds[34]

The following bonds are classified as "qualified tax-credit bonds": qualified forestry conservation bonds, New CREBs, qualified energy conservation bonds and QZABs issued after the date of enactment of the Tax Extenders and Alternative Minimum Tax Relief Act of 2008. Unlike tax-exempt bonds, qualified tax-credit bonds generally are not interest-bearing obligations. Rather, the taxpayer holding a qualified tax-credit bond on a credit allowance date is entitled to a tax credit. The amount of the credit is determined by multiplying the bond's credit rate by the face amount on the holder's bond. The credit rate for an issue of qualified tax credit bonds is determined by the Secretary and is estimated to be a rate that permits issuance of the qualified tax-credit bonds without discount and interest cost to the qualified issuer.[35] The credit accrues quarterly and is includible in gross income (as if it were an interest payment on the bond), and can be claimed against regular income tax liability and alternative minimum tax liability. Unused credits may be carried forward to succeeding taxable years. In addition, credits may be separated from the ownership of the underlying bond similar to how interest coupons can be stripped for interest-bearing bonds.

Qualified tax-credit bonds are subject to a maximum maturity limitation. The maximum maturity is the term which the Secretary estimates will result in the present value of the obligation to repay the principal on a qualified tax-credit bond being equal to 50 percent of the face amount of such bond. The discount rate used to determine the present value amount is the average annual interest rate of tax-exempt obligations having a term of 10 years or more which are issued during the month the qualified tax-credit bonds are issued.

For qualified tax-credit bonds, 100 percent of the available project proceeds must be used within the three-year period that begins on the date of issuance. Available project proceeds are proceeds from the sale of the bond issue less issuance costs (not to exceed two percent) and any investment earnings on such sale proceeds. To the extent less than 100 percent of the available project proceeds are used to finance qualified projects during the three-year spending period, bonds will continue to qualify as qualified tax-credit bonds if unspent proceeds are used within 90 days from the end of such three-year period to redeem bonds. The three-year spending period may be extended by the Secretary upon the qualified issuer's request demonstrating that the failure to satisfy the three-year requirement is due to reasonable cause and the projects will continue to proceed with due diligence.

Qualified tax-credit bonds also are subject to the arbitrage requirements of section 148 that apply to traditional tax-exempt bonds. Principles under section 148 and the regulations thereunder apply for purposes of determining the yield restriction and arbitrage rebate requirements applicable to qualified tax-credit bonds. However, available project proceeds invested during the three-year spending period are not subject to the arbitrage restrictions (i.e., yield restriction and rebate requirements). In addition, amounts invested in a reserve fund are not subject to the arbitrage restrictions to the extent: (1) such fund is funded at a rate not more rapid than equal annual installments; (2) such fund is funded in a manner reasonably expected to result in an amount not greater than an amount necessary to repay the issue; and (3) the yield on such fund is not greater than the average annual interest rate of tax-exempt obligations having a term of 10 years or more that are issued during the month the qualified tax-credit bonds are issued.

Issuers of qualified tax-credit bonds are required to report issuance to the IRS in a manner similar to the information returns required for tax-exempt bonds. In addition, issuers of qualified tax-credit bonds are required to certify that applicable State and local law requirements governing conflicts of interest are satisfied with respect to such issue, and if the Secretary prescribes additional conflicts of interest rules governing the appropriate Members of Congress, Federal, State, and local officials, and their spouses, such additional rules are satisfied with respect to such issue.

III. Benefits and Costs of Tax-Exempt Bond and Tax-Credit Bond Financing

A. Tax-Exempt Bonds

Benefits and Costs of the Subsidy

Issuer Benefit

Tax-exempt financing provides an implicit Federal subsidy to the borrower (i.e., either the qualified governmental unit or the conduit borrower) but, in practice some of the subsidy redounds to the bond investor (the lender). Because interest income on the bonds is excluded from gross income, the bond investor is willing to accept a lower interest rate on the bonds than he might otherwise accept on an identical taxable investment. Thus, the borrower receives an implicit Federal subsidy equal to the difference between the tax-exempt interest rate paid and the taxable rate that otherwise would be paid. In this way, the income exclusion lowers the cost of capital for the State and local governments (or private parties in the case of private activity bonds).

The following example illustrates the Federal subsidy measured as a percentage of the otherwise applicable taxable rate. Assume a school district may borrow either at a taxable rate of 6.25 percent or a tax-exempt rate of 4.5 percent. The yield spread in this example is 1.75 percentage points and the ratio of tax-exempt to taxable rates is 0.72, or 72 percent, and the subsidy is equal to 28 percent of the otherwise applicable taxable rate.[36] To illustrate the benefit of the subsidy in dollar terms, if the school district borrows $1 million at the taxable rate of 6.25 percent and $1 million at the tax-exempt rate of 4.5 percent, the school district's annual interest payments would be $62,500 on the taxable debt, but $45,000 on the tax-exempt debt, a $17,500 savings. In practice, however, this calculation overstates the borrower's interest savings because of certain inefficiencies associated with the issuance of tax-exempt bonds (explained below).

Finally, as the ratio of tax-exempt rates to taxable rates moves closer to one (i.e., the spread between tax-exempt and taxable interest rates narrows), the value of the subsidy to the borrower also diminishes. Among other reasons, this may occur as the volume of tax-exempt bond issuances increases and tax-exempt borrowers respond by offering higher interest rates to attract bond investors. (See Figure 1.a., below, comparing the average tax-exempt interest rate on high-grade municipal bonds and the average taxable interest rate on corporate bonds for the period 1986-2007. Figure 1 .b., below separately reports the yield spread between the interest rates on tax-exempt and taxable bonds).

Bond Investor Benefit

The bond investor also receives a Federal subsidy from tax-exempt financing equal to the difference between the tax-exempt interest rate and the after-tax yield on a taxable investment. The bond investor's willingness to purchase tax-exempt bonds also depends on the bond investor's marginal tax rate. Generally, all other things being equal (such as credit worthiness), a bond investor is indifferent between a tax-exempt bond and a taxable bond with an equivalent after-tax yield.[37] To illustrate using the example from above, if a bond investor with a 28-percent marginal tax rate purchased a $1 million taxable bond at a 6.25-percent rate, as an alternative to the tax-exempt bond, the investor would receive $62,500 in interest income and pay $17,500 in income tax for a net return of $45,000 and an after-tax yield of 4.5 percent. This is the same net return the bond investor receives if he were to purchase the $1 million tax-exempt bond. Thus, this bond investor generally would be indifferent to a taxable investment with a 6.25-percent rate and a tax-exempt investment with a 4.5-percent rate.

With many bond investors in different tax brackets, bond investors in higher marginal tax-brackets receive a larger tax benefit than those in lower brackets. For example, if a bond investor with a 33-percent marginal tax rate purchased the alternative $1 million taxable bond at a 6.25-percent rate, the investor would receive $62,500 in interest income and pay $20,625 in income tax for a net return of $41,875 and an after-tax yield of 4.19 percent. However, this bond investor would receive a 4.5 percent net return on the school district's tax-exempt bond. Thus, unlike the bond investor in the 28-percent marginal tax rate who is indifferent to investment in taxable or tax-exempt bonds, the bond investor in the 33-percent marginal tax rate receives a greater benefit by purchasing the tax-exempt bond. In contrast, a bond investor with a 15- percent marginal tax rate receives no benefit from purchasing the tax-exempt bond.

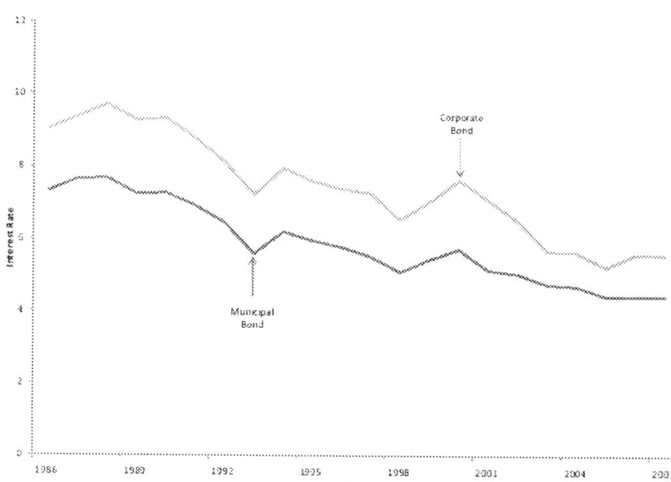

Figure 1.a. Comparison of Long Term Municipal Bond Interest Rates and Corporate Bond Interest Rates, 1986- 2007

Figure 1.b. Yield Spread Between Long Term Municipal Bonds and Corporate Bonds, 1986-2007

Revenue Loss Associated with Tax-Exempt Bonds

The direct cost to the Federal government of the interest exclusion for State and local bonds is the income tax revenue forgone. Under our example, if the bond investor with a 28-percent marginal tax rate purchases the school district's $1 million tax-exempt bond with a 4.5-percent interest rate, the bond investor receives $45,000 of tax-exempt interest income for each year the bond is outstanding. However, assuming the bond investor's preferred alternative investment is a taxable bond, the actual revenue loss to the Federal government is based upon the taxable yield the bond investor forgoes. For example, if the bond investor purchased the taxable bond at a 6.25-percent rate, rather than the tax-exempt bond, the bond investor would have received $62,500 in interest income and paid $17,500 in income tax. In this case, the revenue forgone to the Federal Government equals the interest savings of the school district.

However, using the second part of the example from above, if the bond investor in the 33-percent bracket purchases the school district's tax-exempt bond, it costs the Federal Government $20,625 ($62,500 of interest income taxed at a 33-percent rate). Due to the existence of multiple tax brackets, the loss of Federal receipts is greater than the reduction in the tax-exempt issuer's interest cost. In this case, the $17,500 interest subsidy realized by the school district costs the Federal Government $20,625. The difference accrues to bond investors in tax brackets higher than those that would be implied by the yield spread between taxable and tax- exempt bonds. Thus, if a bond investor in the 28-percent bracket finds it profitable to hold a tax- exempt security, a bond investor in the 33-percent bracket will find it even more profitable. This implies that the Federal Government will lose more in revenue than the tax-exempt issuer gains in reduced interest payments.[38] This is one source of inefficiency to the subsidy provided by the tax exemption.

Table 1, below, reports the data used for Figures 1.a. and 1 .b. It also calculates the implied marginal tax rate at which the bond investor would be indifferent between holding the average corporate bond and the average municipal bond.[39] The table shows that generally over the past two decades any holdings of tax-exempt bonds by bond investors in a 25-percent marginal tax bracket and above would have led to the inefficiency described above.[40]

Issuance Costs

Borrowers always incur transactions costs in attaining loanable funds. Generally, issuing tax-exempt bonds to finance capital costs is a complex and expensive process. In addition to the borrower and bond investor, there are a number of parties employed to facilitate a bond issuance (e.g., service providers such as investment bankers and attorneys). The requirements for tax exemption may result in higher incremental costs of issuance for tax-exempt bonds than those associated with issuing taxable bonds. Because a portion of the benefits of tax exemption flows to these service providers in the way of fees, such fees are a second potential source of inefficiency resulting from tax-exempt financing.

Arbitrage Potential

As described in Part II.D, above, present law generally restricts the ability of qualified governmental units and other parties to earn and retain arbitrage profits. Without these rules, the reduced cost of funds obtained through tax-exempt bonds provides issuers the opportunity to earn arbitrage profits by investing tax-exempt bond proceeds in higher yielding investments. For example, the average yield spread between taxable and tax-exempt debt for the period 1986- 2007, as reported in Table 1, above, was approximately 1.6 percent. Consider a simple arbitrage transaction of the type available to borrowers using tax-exempt debt prior to restrictions adopted by the Congress in 1969. Assume a local government planned to construct a $10 million building. Further assume the local government issued $10 million in tax-exempt bonds with the knowledge that the construction schedule was such that the local government could invest a five- year average of $5 million of the $10 million in bond proceeds in taxable securities yielding interest at 1.00 percent greater than the interest the issuer would owe on its tax-exempt bonds. This investment would generate $50,000 in profit to the local governmental issuer annually net of interest payments to the owners of the local government's bonds.[41] Over the five-year period, the quarter of million dollar profit equals 2.5 percent of principal value of the bond issue. The ability to earn arbitrage profits means that project costs are lowered beyond the benefit reflected in a comparison of taxable and tax-exempt interest rates. One could say that, if the yield spread reflects the implicit Federal subsidy to a State or local issuer's borrowing costs, potential arbitrage profits reflect an implicit Federal subsidy to the payment of the principal amount of the State or local issuer's borrowing.

Table 1. Comparison of Taxable Interest Rates and Tax-Exempt Interest Rates, 1986-2007

Year	Corporate Bonds [1] [Percent]	High-Grade Municipal Bonds [2] [Percent]	Yield Spread [Percent]	Implied Tax Rate of Marginal Investor [Percent]
1986	9.02	7.33	1.69	18.7
1987	9.38	7.66	1.72	18.3
1988	9.71	7.68	2.03	20.9
1989	9.26	7.23	2.03	21.9
1990	9.32	7.27	2.05	22.0
1991	8.77	6.92	1.85	21.1
1992	8.14	6.44	1.70	20.9
1993	7.22	5.59	1.63	22.6
1994	7.96	6.19	1.77	22.2
1995	7.59	5.95	1.64	21.6
1996	7.37	5.76	1.61	21.8
1997	7.26	5.52	1.74	24.0
1998	6.53	5.09	1.44	22.1
1999	7.04	5.44	1.60	22.7
2000	7.62	5.71	1.91	25.1
2001	7.08	5.15	1.93	27.3
2002	6.49	5.04	1.45	22.3
2003	5.67	4.74	0.93	16.4
2004	5.63	4.68	0.95	16.9
2005	5.24	4.40	0.84	16.0
2006	5.59	4.40	1.19	21.3
2007	5.56	4.40	1.16	20.9

[1] Annual average bond yield for Moody's Long Term Aaa Corporate Bond Index. Source: *Economic Report of the President, 2008.*

[2] Bond Buyer 20-year Municipal Bond Index, an index consisting of 20 general obligation bonds that mature in 20 years. The average rating of the bonds is roughly equivalent to Moody's Aa1 rating. Source: *2008 Thompson Financial Bond Buyer Year Book*.

Arbitrage transactions have no economic substance, as the issuance of one financial instrument (the tax-exempt bond) is offset by the purchase of another financial instrument (typically another debt instrument). The transaction is made profitable solely through the ability to borrow at tax-exempt rates in reliance on a Federal subsidy of borrowing costs. If permitted to earn and retain arbitrage profits, borrowers would have a substantial incentive to issue more bonds, to issue them earlier, and to leave them outstanding longer than necessary. From the Federal Government's standpoint, allowing arbitrage profits to be earned from the issuance of tax-exempt bonds is an inefficient alternative to additional borrowing, because it is more costly to the Federal Government in terms of forgone tax revenue than the additional borrowing that would be necessary to produce the same amount of proceeds.

More Recent Market Conditions for Tax-Exempt Debt

With recent financial market turmoil the value of Federal tax exemption has declined. Figure 2, below, makes the same comparison as does Figure 1, comparing the average yield on 20-year general obligation tax-exempt bonds to roughly comparable 20-year taxable bonds. Figure 2 reports bond yields monthly on the middle Thursday of each month. In both September and October of 2008, the market has priced the implicit subsidy from tax-exempt borrowing at less than 11 percent.

Figures 1 and 2 have reported bond yields on long-term bonds. State and local issuers also issue short-term debt, such as exempt commercial paper. Like taxable enterprises, State and local governments use short-term borrowing to finance payroll and other current budget needs that are not perfectly matched to timing of their tax revenues. Figure 3, below, compares yields for 30-day tax-exempt commercial paper to yields on 30-day Aa rated nonfinancial commercial paper.[42] Figure 3 documents that the yield spread between taxable and tax-exempt commercial paper has narrowed significantly over the past 12 months. In October 2008, tax-exempt commercial paper traded at a yield in excess of that of taxable commercial paper, notwithstanding the tax exemption available.

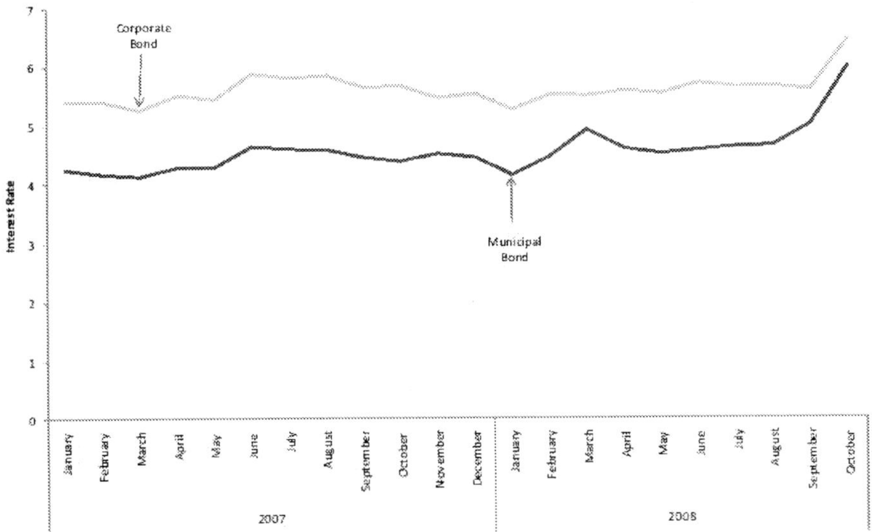

Figure 2. Comparison of Long Term Municipal Bond Investment Rates and Corporate Bond Internet Rates, Monthly 2007 and 2008

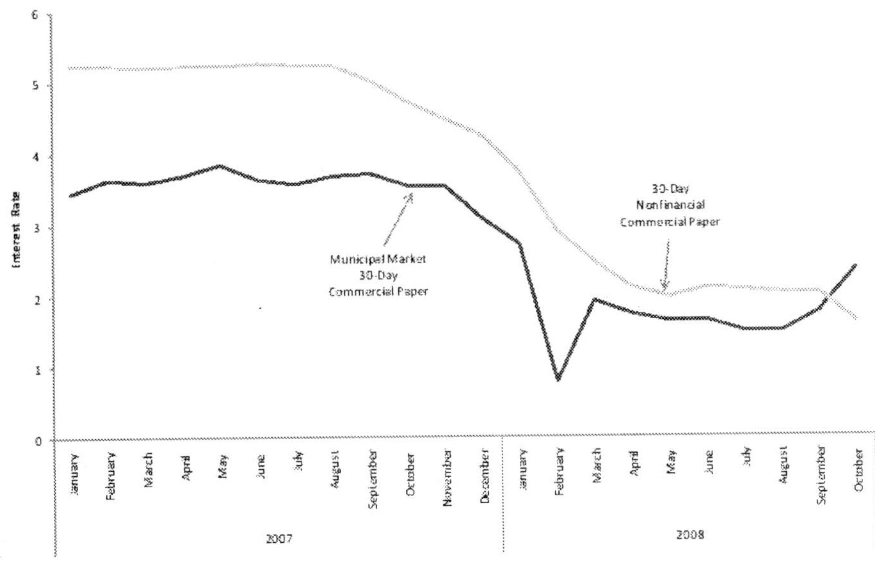

Figure 3. Comparison of Yields on Tax-Exempt and Taxable Commercial Paper Monthly 2007 and 2008

B. Tax-Credit Bonds

Benefits and Costs of the Subsidy[43]

One Hundred Percent Interest Credit

As described above, tax-credit bonds that have been issued to date are not interest-bearing obligations. Rather, the taxpayer holding a tax-credit bond on a credit allowance date is entitled to a tax credit. The amount of the credit is determined by multiplying the bond's credit rate by the face amount[44] on the holder's bond. For the present law categories of tax-credit bonds, the credit rate on the bonds is determined by the Secretary of the Treasury and is an estimate of the rate that permits issuance of such bonds without discount and interest cost to the qualified issuer. That is, the tax credit is chosen to approximate an interest rate subsidy of 100 percent. The credit is includible in gross income (as if it were an interest payment on the bond), and can be claimed against regular income tax liability and alternative minimum tax liability.

Under present law, the Federal subsidy provided to issuers by tax-credit bonds is deeper than the subsidy for tax-exempt bonds. This is because the issuer of tax-credit bonds pays no interest, only principal.[45] The "interest" is paid by the Federal Government in the form of tax credits. Thus, the issuer theoretically has an interest-free loan. In comparison, issuers of tax- exempt bonds pay interest on such obligations, albeit at a lower interest rate than if the debt were taxable. As noted above, the Federal subsidy provided to borrowers using tax-exempt bonds is limited to the difference between the tax-exempt interest rate paid and the taxable bond rate that otherwise would be paid.[46]

The Federal subsidy for tax-credit bonds is economically equivalent to the Federal government directly paying the interest on a taxable bond issue on behalf of the State or local government benefiting from the bond proceeds.[47] To see this, consider any taxable bond that bears an interest rate of 10 percent. A thousand dollar bond would thus produce an interest payment of $100 annually. The owner of the bond that receives this payment would receive a net payment of $100 less the taxes owed on that interest. If the taxpayer were in the 28-percent Federal tax bracket, such taxpayer would receive $72 after Federal taxes. Regardless of whether the State government or the Federal government pays the interest, the taxpayer receives the same net-of-tax return of $72. In the case of tax-credit bonds, no cash interest is paid by the Federal government. Rather, a tax credit of $100 is allowed to be taken by the holder of the bond. In general, a $100 tax credit would be worth $100 to a taxpayer, provided that the taxpayer had at least $100 in tax liability. However, for tax-credit bonds, the $100 credit also has to be claimed as income. Claiming an additional $100 in income costs a taxpayer in the 28-percent tax bracket an additional $28 in income taxes, payable to the Federal government. With the $100 tax credit that is ultimately claimed, the taxpayer nets $72 of interest income by holding the bond. The Federal government loses $100 on the credit, but recoups $28 of that by the requirement that it be included in income, for a net cost of $72, which is exactly the net return to the taxpayer. If the Federal government had simply agreed to pay the interest on behalf of the State or local government, both the Federal government and the bondholder/taxpayer would be in the same situation. The Federal government would make outlays of $100 in interest payments, but would recoup $28 of that in tax receipts, for a net budgetary cost of $72, as before. Similarly, the bondholder/taxpayer would receive a taxable $100 in interest, and would owe $28 in taxes, for a net gain of $72, as before. The State or local government also would be in the same situation in both cases.

In addition to the deeper subsidy provided by 100-percent tax credit bonds, tax-credit bonds do not generate the same revenue loss inefficiency as do tax-exempt bonds. As explained in Part III.A., above, in the case of a tax-exempt bond, the loss of Federal receipts is greater than the reduction in the tax-exempt issuer's interest cost. This is due to the existence of multiple tax brackets and the bond investor's tax saving is dependent upon the bond investor's marginal tax rate. With a tax-credit bond, the bond investor's tax saving is independent of the bond investor's marginal tax rate. As a consequence, with a tax-credit bond, the loss in Federal receipts from the tax credit equals the reduction in the tax-credit bond issuer's interest cost.

Partial Tax-Credit Bonds

As explained above, present-law tax-credit bonds attempt to offer a 100-percent interest rate subsidy. A tax-credit bond need not be structured as solely an instrument that offers a 100-percent interest subsidy. The Energy Improvement and Extension Act of 2008 authorizes the Treasury to allocate $800 million in new CREBs and $800 million in qualified energy conservation bonds that will carry a tax-credit equal to 70 percent of a 100-percent tax-credit bond. As such bonds have not yet been issued, it is unclear if issuers will choose to supplement the bond with a cash coupon such that the bond will initially sell at par or merely rely on the proceeds of a bond that likely would sell at a discount to par. Other analysts have suggested a different structure in which issuers would issue tax-credit bonds that have a cash interest component, the interest income of which would be taxable, and that a tax credit also may be claimed for receipt of such cash interest payments.[48]

As reported in Table 1, above, tax-exempt debt generally has offered borrowers an interest rate subsidy of 25 percent or less for the past two decades. Because the additional revenue cost to the Federal government that arises as a result of the current income tax structure's increasing marginal tax rates does not arise when individuals or institutions hold tax- credit bonds rather than tax-exempt bonds (a credit generally has the same value regardless of a taxpayer's marginal tax rate), it may be possible to choose a credit rate that provides an interest rate subsidy of greater than 25 percent (but substantially less than 100 percent) and cost the Federal government less in forgone revenue than would the issuance of a traditional tax-exempt bond for the same State or local purpose.

Issuance Costs and Arbitrage Potential

Issuance Costs

At present, issuance costs for tax-credit bonds likely exceed those of tax-exempt bonds. Because tax-credit bonds are relatively new financial instruments, fewer potential borrowers are familiar with the applicable rules. Also, present law limits the total dollar value of issuance of these instruments. This, too, would likely discourage participation by some service providers (*i.e.*, investment bankers, financial advisors, and bond counsel). These factors generally would result in fewer service providers competing for the business of helping borrowers issue tax-credit debt, with the result being higher prices for such services. Because a portion of the benefit of the tax credit flows to these service providers in the way of fees, such fees are a second potential source of inefficiency resulting from tax-exempt financing. Through time more service providers would be expected to become familiar with these financial instruments reducing current disparities in the issuance costs of tax-exempt and tax-credit bonds. If the Congress were to continue to permit the issuance of tax-credit bonds, their increased share in the financial market also would be expected to reduce current disparities in the issuance costs of tax-exempt and tax-credit bonds. Nevertheless, as is the case with tax-exempt bonds, the additional requirements for tax-credit bonds may result in higher incremental costs of issuance for tax-credit bonds than those associated with issuing taxable bonds.

Arbitrage Potential

In general tax-credit bonds are subject to the same arbitrage and rebate requirements, as detailed in section 148 of the Code, applicable to tax-exempt State and local bonds. However, issuers of QZABs, new CREBs, qualified energy conservation bonds, and forestry conservation bonds are allowed to take advantage of special arbitrage rules that provide a limited ability for borrowers to invest bond proceeds and use the earnings from such investments to make additional qualified expenditures. This ability to invest bond proceeds and retain the earnings increases the magnitude of the tax expenditure available for qualified expenditure purposes beyond the interest cost saving achieved through having the borrower's interest costs paid in full, or in part, by the Federal tax credit. If as a general matter issuers of tax-credit bonds had the ability to earn and retain arbitrage profits, issuers would have an incentive to issue more tax- credit bonds and to issue the bonds earlier than necessary to fund a qualified project. As a result, there may be increased delays in the expenditure of bond proceeds for approved purposes to earn greater arbitrage profits.

End Notes

[1] This document may be cited as follows: Joint Committee on Taxation, *Present Law and Issues Related to Infrastructure Finance* (JCX-83-08), October 24, 2008. This document can also be found on our website at www.jct.gov.

[2] In order to be tax-exempt, such bonds must also satisfy any applicable State and local laws (*e.g.*, because some States prohibit the issuance of public debt with the full faith and credit of the issuer for private purposes many private activity bonds are not general obligations of the issuer but revenue bonds).

[3] Unless otherwise stated, all section references are to the Internal Revenue Code of 1986, as amended (the "Code") and all regulation references are to the Treasury Regulations promulgated thereunder.

[4] Sec. 141.

[5] The 10 percent private business test is reduced to five percent in the case of private business uses (and payments with respect to such uses) that are unrelated to any governmental use being financed by the issue.

[6] Treas. Reg. sec. 1.141-3(b)(4).

[7] Treas. Reg. sec. 1.141-4(c)(3).

[8] Sec. 141(e).

[9] Sec. 142(a).

[10] Sec. 142(a)(11) and sec. 142(i).

[11] A metropolitan statistical area for this purpose is defined by reference to section 143(k)(2)(B). Under that provision, the term metropolitan statistical area includes the area defined as such by the Secretary of Commerce.

[12] Sec. 142(i)(2).

[13] Sec. 142(i)(3).

[14] Sec. 146(g)(4).

[15] As of July 14, 2008, the Department of Transportation had made the following allocations of the $15 billion in qualified highway or surface freight transfer facility bond authority:

Project	Allocation (millions of dollars)
Port of Miami Tunnel, Consortium Miami Access Tunnel	980.0
Missouri DOT Safe and Sound Bridge Improvement Project	700.0
Knik Arm Crossing, Alaska	600.0
Virginia I-495 Capital Beltway HOT Lanes	589.0
Texas Department of Transportation Interstate Highway 635 (LBJ Freeway)	288.0
Pennsylvania Turnpike Capital Improvements	2,000.0
Ambassador Bridge Gateway Project - Phase I (Detroit, Michigan -Windsor, Ontario, Canada	212.6
Total approved allocations as of 7/14/08	5,369.6

Source: Federal Highway Administration

[16] Sec. 144(b)(1).

[17] The "Gulf Opportunity Zone" is defined as that portion of the Hurricane Katrina Disaster Area determined by the President to warrant individual or individual and public assistance from the Federal Government under the Robert T. Stafford Disaster Relief and Emergency Assistance Act by reason of Hurricane Katrina.

[18] The "Midwestern disaster area" is defined as an area with respect to which a major disaster was declared by the President on or after May 20, 2008, and before August 1, 2008, under section 401 of the Robert T. Stafford Disaster Relief and Emergency Assistance Act ("Stafford Act") by reason of severe storms, tornados, or flooding occurring in any of the States of Arkansas, Illinois, Indiana, Iowa, Kansas, Michigan, Minnesota, Missouri, Nebraska, and Wisconsin, and determined by the President to warrant individual or individual and public assistance from the Federal government under such Act with respect to damages attributable to such severe storms, tornados, or flooding. For certain provisions, areas eligible for only public assistance are included in the definition of Midwestern disaster area.

[19] The "Hurricane Ike disaster area" is defined as an area in the State of Texas or Louisiana with respect to which a major disaster has been declared by the President on September 13, 2008, under section 401 of the Stafford Act by reason of Hurricane Ike, and determined by the President to warrant individual or individual and public assistance from the Federal government under such Act with respect to damages attributable to Hurricane Ike.

[20] Sec. 1394(b).

[21] Sec. 1397C.

[22] Sec. 146.

[23] Sec. 146(f)(5).

[24] Sec. 147(b).

[25] Sec. 147(h).

[26] Treas. Reg. sec. 5f.103-2(g)(3).

[27] Secs. 103(a) and (b)(2).

[28] For example, a tax-exempt issuer might be able to borrow money at six percent and invest the funds in taxable securities that yield eight percent. The tax exempt issuer would earn a profit of two percent. This two-percent profit is, in effect, a subsidy from the Federal government to the tax-exempt issuer. The arbitrage restrictions are necessary to control this subsidy.

[29] Sec. 149(d)(5).

[30] Sec. 149(d)(3). Bonds issued before 1986 and pursuant to certain transition rules contained in the Tax Reform Act of 1986 may be advance refunded more than one time in certain cases.

[31] Sec. 149(d)(2). Special rules apply for certain advance refundings in the New York Liberty Zone and the Gulf Opportunity Zone.

[32] The exceptions include guarantees by: the Federal Housing Administration, the Department of Veterans' Affairs, the Federal National Mortgage Association, the Federal Home Loan Mortgage Association, the Government National Mortgage Association; the Student Loan Marketing Association; and the Bonneville Power Authority pursuant to the Northwest Power Act (16 U.S.C. sec. 839d). The exception also includes guarantees for certain housing programs. These are: (a) private activity bonds for a qualified residential rental project or a housing program obligation under section 11(b) of the United States Housing Act of 1937; (b) a qualified mortgage bond; or (c) a qualified veterans' mortgage bond. In addition, if certain requirements are met, the Federal guarantee prohibition does not apply to any guarantee by a Federal home loan bank made in connection with the original issuance of a bond during the period July 30, 2008 through December 31, 2010.

[33] Sec. 149(e).

[34] Separate rules apply in the case of tax-credit bonds which are not qualified tax-credit bonds (e.g., "old QZABs," "Gulf tax-credit bonds," "Midwestern tax-credit bonds," and "old CREBs").

[35] However, for New CREBs and qualified energy conservation bonds, the applicable credit rate is 70 percent of the otherwise applicable rate.

[36] Column 5 of Table 1, on page 28, may be used to illustrate the measure of the subsidy measured as a percentage of the otherwise applicable taxable rate for the period 1986-2007.

[37] This may be represented as $r_e = (1-t)r$, where r_e is the tax-exempt yield, t is the investor's marginal tax rate, and r is the taxable bond yield.

[38] To the extent that bond investors in lower tax brackets purchase tax-exempt bonds for nontax reasons, such as to help support the local schools, the revenue forgone would be less than the issuer's interest savings.

[39] Some analysts suggest that consideration of other financial assets beyond a comparison of taxable and tax-exempt bonds determine the yield spread between taxable and tax-exempt interest rates. In particular, these analysts suggest that the yield spread increases (decreases) as the dividend yield on corporate stocks increases (decreases). (N. Gregory Mankiw and James M. Poterba, "Stock Market Yields and the Pricing of Municipal Bonds," National Bureau of Economic Research Working Paper #5 607, June 1996.) However, such an augmented analysis of the yield spread does not alter the conclusion that the Federal Government loses more in revenue from State and local issuance of tax- exempt bonds, than the borrower gains in reduced interest costs.

[40] Individual taxpayers are asked to self-report tax-exempt interest income earned during the taxable year, although there is no penalty for a failure to report (*e.g.*, line 8a of Form 1040). The staff of the Joint Committee on Taxation projects that for 2009 approximately 4.9 million individual taxpayers will report approximately $71 billion of tax-exempt interest. Of those totals, the staff of the Joint Committee on Taxation projects that 3.2 million taxpayers will be in marginal tax brackets of 25 percent or higher in 2009 and they will report in excess of $56 billion in tax-exempt interest.

[41] For simple examples and explanations of arbitrage transactions, see, Dennis Zimmerman, *The Private Use of Tax-Exempt Bonds*, (Washington, D.C.: The Urban Institute Press), 1991, pp. 158-162.

[42] The source for yields on tax-exempt commercial paper in Figure 3 is Municipal Market Data. The source for yields on nonfinancial commercial paper is the Federal Reserve. The data in Figure 3 represent the quoted yields reported on the middle Friday of each month.

[43] Congressional Budget Office, *Tax-Credit Bonds and the Federal Cost of Financing Public Expenditures*, July 2004, offers an analysis of the economics of tax-credit bonds and alternatives.

[44] The "face amount" (or par value) represents the value of a bond at maturity as stated on the bond certificate.

[45] This conclusion assumes the bonds are not issued at discount. If tax-credit bonds are issued at discount, *i.e.*, less than par value, the issuer incurs interest cost to the extent its debt service payments will exceed the amount of proceeds received from the sale of the bonds. This may occur because the rate on a prospective issue of tax-credit bonds is set lower than what investors are willing to accept to purchase the bonds at par value. To illustrate, assume the credit rate on tax-credit bonds with a face amount of $100 is set at five percent. If investors do not view the five percent credit rate as an acceptable return given the riskiness of the investment, they will purchase the bonds for something less than $100, *e.g.*, $90. Because the credit is determined by reference to the face amount of bonds ($100), the investor purchasing tax- credit bonds at a discount ($90) receives a higher yield than the stated credit rate. However, the issuer must repay the full face value of the bonds, $100 in this example, even though it received less than $100 in proceeds.

[46] This discussion ignores any potential for permitted arbitrage earnings.

[47] This is true provided that the taxpayer faces tax liability of at least the amount of the credit. Without sufficient tax liability, the proposed tax-credit arrangement would not be as advantageous. Presumably, only taxpayers who anticipate having sufficient tax liability to be offset by the proposed credit would hold these bonds.

[48] One such vision of a partial tax-credit bond is described in CBO, *Tax-Credit Bonds and the Federal Cost of Financing Public Expenditures*.

In: Role of Tax Preferences in Financial... ISBN: 978-1-61668-546-1
Editors: Michael D. Scott

Chapter 3

Subsidizing Infrastructure Investment with Tax-Preferred Bonds

Congressional Budget Office and Joint Committee on Taxation Study

Summary

The public and private sectors in the United States together spend over $500 billion a year on infrastructure projects, including highways and airports, water and energy utilities, dams, waste-disposal sites and other environmental facilities, schools, and hospitals. The federal government makes a significant contribution to that investment through its direct expenditures and the subsidies it provides indirectly through the tax system, which are sometimes referred to as **tax expenditures**. Direct expenditures comprise what the federal government spends on infrastructure (for example, by funding construction of dams and other water resources by the Army Corps of Engineers) and what it provides as grants and loan subsidies to states and localities (primarily for transportation projects). Those expenditures and grants account for a bit more than one-eighth of the roughly half-trillion dollars in total capital expenditures on infrastructure in the United States. However, for specific types of projects—for example, transportation and environmental facilities—those outlays represent about one-half or more of the total investment.

The Importance of Tax Preferences in Financing Infrastructure

Most federal tax expenditures for infrastructure are the result of tax preferences granted for bonds that state and local governments issue to finance capital spending on infrastructure. For fiscal years 2008 to 2012, federal revenues forgone through the tax-exempt bond financing of infrastructure—both for new investments and for the refinancing of existing debt—are estimated to exceed $26 billion annually.

Tax preferences for bonds reduce borrowing costs. Because infrastructure facilities typically provide a stream of benefits (and, in some cases, revenues) well into the future, their construction is often financed by borrowing.

The amount of tax-preferred debt issued to finance new infrastructure projects undertaken by the public and private sectors totaled $1.7 trillion from 1991 to 2007. About three-quarters of those bond proceeds, or roughly $1.3 trillion, was for capital spending on infrastructure by states and localities, and the remainder was used to fund private capital investment for projects that serve a public purpose, such as schools and hospitals. That $1.3 trillion amounted to over one-half of the $2.3 trillion in capital spending on infrastructure by state and local governments (that is, net of federal grants and loan subsidies). Since 1991, tax-exempt bonds have become a more important source of financing, particularly for public investment in transportation facilities, such as highways, and for private investment in schools.

Tax preferences for debt are also attractive to states and localities because they generally allow those governments to exercise broad discretion over the types of projects they finance and the amount of debt they issue. But unlike direct expenditures, tax expenditures—including tax preferences for state and local bonds (also known as municipal bonds)—are not subject to the annual appropriation process that determines federal outlays for infrastructure and other discretionary programs. As a result, the cost of tax subsidies for infrastructure is not readily apparent, making the design of cost-effective tax preferences all the more important.

That history and the projected demand for investment in the nation's infrastructure draw attention to the question of how to make the most effective use of the range of policy options available to support investment in infrastructure. Understanding the advantages and disadvantages of the various types of tax preferences and their role in financing infrastructure investment is an important issue in that regard.

The Types of Tax-Preferred Bonds and Their Characteristics

The Internal Revenue Code provides for three forms of tax-preferred state and local bonds:

- **Tax-exempt bonds** pay interest to the bondholder that is not subject to federal income tax.
- **Tax-credit bonds,** by contrast, generally provide a credit against the bondholder's overall federal income tax liability.
- **Direct-pay tax-credit bonds,** in effect, require the federal government to make cash payments to the issuer of the bond in an amount equal to a portion of each of the interest payments the issuer makes to the bondholder.

Tax-exempt bonds are the most well established type of tax-preferred debt (tax exemption dates to the beginning of the federal income tax in 1913) and are issued to finance either the general functions of state and local governments or certain projects undertaken by the private sector. Tax-exempt bonds reduce the issuer's borrowing costs because purchasers of such debt are willing to accept a lower rate of interest than that of taxable debt of comparable risk and maturity.[1] However, tax-exempt bonds are a relatively costly mechanism for delivering a subsidy to the issuer of the bonds, because the revenue forgone by the federal government in connection with the tax exemption is not limited to the issuer's subsidy; a portion of the federal subsidy is captured by holders of tax- exempt bonds whose tax rates exceed the rate of tax on the marginal (or market-clearing) buyers of the tax- exempt bonds.[2]

In contrast to tax-exempt bonds, **tax-credit bonds** are much more recent in origin. Authority for the first tax- credit bonds, known as Qualified Zone Academy Bonds, was added to the Internal Revenue Code in 1997, effective for 1998. Although the outstanding amount of tax-credit bonds currently is minuscule in comparison with that of tax-exempt bonds, tax-credit bonds potentially offer two advantages for economic efficiency. First, tax- credit bonds can be a more cost-effective means of subsidizing borrowing, because every dollar of federal revenue forgone through the tax credit is transferred to borrowers rather than accruing to individuals whose marginal tax rate is high. Second, although tax-credit bonds have tended to provide a subsidy that is close to 100 percent of interest costs, the amount of the tax credit can be adjusted, depending on the purpose for which the bonds are issued. By adjusting the credit amount, the Congress effectively can exempt more or less of each dollar of interest income on a bond and tailor the federal subsidy to the public benefit the Congress expects to derive from the project being subsidized.

Nevertheless, tax-credit bond programs have not been particularly well received by the market for a number of reasons, including the limited size and temporary nature of tax-credit bond programs and the absence of rules for separating tax credits from the associated bonds and reselling them. That situation is likely to change, however, as a result of the American Recovery and Reinvestment Act of 2009 (ARRA, Public Law 111-5), which greatly expanded the size and range of tax-credit bond programs. As those new programs are implemented, it will be possible to gauge more accurately the practical advantages and disadvantages of tax-credit bonds.

ARRA also created a third type of tax-preferred debt— the **direct-pay tax-credit bond**. With that type of bond, the federal government makes a payment to the issuer in lieu of providing a tax credit to the holder of the bond. For example, issuers of the new Build America Bonds (also authorized by ARRA) can elect to issue direct-pay bonds provided that 100 percent of the available proceeds from the bond are to be used for capital expenditures. The issuer of those bonds receives a payment from the federal government equal to 35 percent of the taxable interest paid to the holder of the bond. In part because the direct payment to the issuer represents a "deeper" subsidy to the issuer than the provision of a tax credit represents to the bondholder, the direct-pay option of qualifying Build America Bonds has been particularly well received by issuers. In addition, fully taxable Build America Bonds must offer yields comparable with those of other taxable securities. Those yields may make the bonds an attractive investment for tax-exempt and foreign persons, who do not invest in traditional tax- exempt bonds.

Conclusions

The estimated $26 billion in annual federal revenue forgone through tax-exempt bond financing of infrastructure is greater than the associated reduction in borrowing costs for state and local governments. Some analysts have estimated the magnitude of that differential and conclude that several billion dollars each year may simply accrue to bondholders in higher income-tax brackets without providing any cost savings to borrowers.

Replacing tax-exempt interest with tax credits could, in principle, increase the efficiency of financing infrastructure with tax-preferred debt. Tax-credit bonds transfer to issuers all of the federal revenues forgone through the tax preference; in addition, the amount of the tax credit can be varied across types of infrastructure projects, thus bringing the federal revenue loss in line with the benefits expected from the investment.

1. Paying for Infrastructure

Investment in the nation's infrastructure each year amounts to roughly a half-trillion dollars. Both government and the private sector fund that investment, which covers the costs of constructing and renovating such facilities as highways and airports, water and energy utilities, dams, waste-disposal and other environmental sites, schools, and hospitals.

The federal government makes a significant contribution to that investment through its direct expenditures and the subsidies it provides indirectly through the tax system. **Direct expenditures** comprise what the federal government spends on infrastructure (for example, by funding construction of dams and other water resources by the Army Corps of Engineers) and what it provides as **grants and loan subsidies** to states and localities (primarily for transportation projects).

Because infrastructure facilities typically provide a stream of benefits (and revenues for repayment) well into the future, their construction is often financed by borrowing. States and localities issue debt to finance projects undertaken by government and, in some cases, by the private sector (bonds issued by states and localities to finance either government operations or certain private-sector activities are known as **municipal bonds**). The federal government subsidizes the issuance of municipal bonds by offering **tax preferences** that lower the cost of debt incurred for those projects.

The substantial need for additional investment in infrastructure has drawn attention to who should pay for any new investment and how that spending might best be financed. Government accounts for the bulk of investment in infrastructure today, largely reflecting the likelihood that infrastructure would otherwise be under-supplied. Recently, however, the private sector has been viewed as an increasingly viable source of financing; from that perspective, a key issue is whether the government should offer incentives (say, through tax subsidies or other favorable regulation) to encourage such investment. This study, prepared jointly by the Congressional Budget Office and the Joint Committee on Taxation, focuses on the use of tax-preferred debt to finance infrastructure. After an overview of investment in infrastructure in the United States—who pays for it, how much it costs, and the federal government's role in financing it—the study:

- Discusses some of the advantages and disadvantages of tax preferences as a means of providing federal financial support for investment in infrastructure;
- Outlines the rules applicable to the issuance of tax- exempt and tax-credit bonds;
- Reviews historical trends in the issuance of tax- preferred bonds and quantifies the reliance of state and local governments and the private sector on such bonds as a means of financing their capital spending; and
- Considers potential efficiency improvements to current tax policy through appropriately structured tax-credit bonds.

Overview of Investment in the Nation's Infrastructure

In this analysis, investment in infrastructure is defined as capital spending on transportation, utilities (for example, water and power supply), environmental projects, and schools.[3] In addition, because they account for a significant share of the tax-exempt debt issued, health care facilities and hospitals are treated as infrastructure in this study, although they might not be classified as such for many other types of analyses. Capital spending under this study's definition consists of investment in physical capital, such as structures and facilities, rather than intangible capital, which is formed by spending on educational programs or on research and development.

Public- and Private-Sector Roles

Investment in infrastructure comes from both public and private sources. The public sector supplies almost all investment in transportation infrastructure (with the exception of freight railroads), water and sewer utilities, and the environment (with the exception of pollution control and waste disposal). The public sector also accounts for about three-quarters of capital spending on education—notably for primary and secondary schools. The private sector provides almost all investment in energy utilities and in health care facilities and hospitals, funds most of the investment in pollution control and waste disposal, and is the sole source of capital spending on freight railroads (see Table 1-1 and Figure 1-1).[4]

Table 1.1. Capital Spending on Types of Infrastructure Financed by Tax-Preferred Bonds, 2007

(Billions of dollars)	Public			Private	Total
	Federal	State and Local	Subtotal		
	Transportation				
Highways	34.4	49.9	84.3	0	84.3
Mass Transit[a]	9.0	4.3	13.3	b	13.3
Freight Railroads	0	0	0	9.6	9.6
Passenger Railroads	0.8[c]	0	0.8	b	0.8
Aviation	6.1	6.4	12.5	1.5	14.0
Water Transportation[d]	1.1	2.2	3.3	1.3	4.6
Subtotal, Transportation	**51.4**	**62.8**	**114.2**	**12.4**	**126.6**
	Utilities				
Drinking and Wastewater	2.3	32.5	34.8	2.8[e]	37.6
Energy[f]	1.4	8.9	10.3	80.8[e]	91.1
Subtotal, Utilities	**3.7**	**41.4**	**45.1**	**83.6**	**128.7**
	Environment				
Water and Other Natural Resources[g]	8.4	5.3	13.7	0	13.7
Pollution Control and Waste Disposalh	0.9	2.0	2.9	5.1[i]	8.0
Subtotal, Environment	**9.3**	**7.3**	**16.6**	**5.1**	**21.7**
(Billions of dollars)	**Public**			**Private**	**Total**
	Federal	**State and Local**	**Subtotal**		
	Other				
Education[j]	0.4	94.0	94.4	27.8[i]	122.2
Health Care[k]	3.4	9.8	13.2	115.0[i]	128.2
Subtotal, Other	**3.8**	**103.8**	**107.6**	**142.8**	**250.4**
Total	**68.2**	**215.3**	**283.5**	**243.9**	**527.4**

Source: Congressional Budget Office based on data from the following sources unless otherwise specified: for federal spending, Congressional Budget Office analysis of data reported in *Budget of the United States Government, Fiscal Year 2009: Analytical Perspectives*, Table 6.2, www.whitehouse.gov/omb/budget; for state and local spending, U.S. Census Bureau, State and Local Government Finances, 2005–2006 and 2006–2007, www.census.gov/govs/estimate; and for private-sector investment, Bureau of Economic Analysis, National Economic Accounts, Fixed Asset Tables, Table 3.7S, www.bea.gov/national/FA2004/TableView.asp?SelectedTable = 55&FirstYear = 2002&LastYear = 2007&Freq = Year. Private spending for transportation equipment is primarily for vehicles, which can be used anywhere in the system and therefore are not considered part of investment in transportation infrastructure.

Notes: Public-sector spending is for federal fiscal year 2007; state and local spending has been estimated to conform to federal fiscal year 2007 and is net of federal grants and loan subsidies realized in that year. Private-sector spending is for calendar year 2007.

Historical data on public spending by federal, state, and local governments on many of the types of infrastructure shown in this table, along with a detailed discussion of data definitions, sources, and methodology, can be found in Congressional Budget Office, *Trends in Public Spending on Transportation and Water Infrastructure*, 1956–2004 (August 2007), and the supporting documentation.

a. Includes subways, bus transportation, and commuter rail.

b. The Bureau of Economic Analysis's Table 3.7S reports $0.8 billion of private investment in structures for "Transit and ground passenger transportation" in 2007; however, that figure includes spending on structures for taxi and limousine services and proprietary and charter bus services, which are not considered as infrastructure in this study.

c. *See Budget of the United States Government, Fiscal Year 2009: Appendix*, pp. 905–906.

d. Includes inland waterways, harbors, and port facilities.

e. Data are from Census Bureau, *2007 Annual Capital Expenditures Survey*, Table 4a, www.census.gov/econ/aces/xls/2007/ Full%20Report.htm.

f. Includes the generation, transmission, and distribution of electricity and the distribution of natural gas.

g. Includes dams and flood control; conservation (of wildlife and forestry, for example); and geological, oceanic, and atmospheric surveys.

h. Includes disposal of hazardous and solid waste.

i. Data are from Bureau of Economic Analysis, National Economic Accounts, Fixed Asset Tables, Table 3.7ES. The data include structures and equipment.

j. Includes primary and secondary schools, colleges and universities, vocational schools, and special education.

k. Includes hospitals, clinics, and other health care facilities and equipment.

Considerations of economic efficiency and equity—that is, ensuring that sufficient infrastructure services are provided and that they are widely available—determine the relative amounts of public- and private-sector investment in infrastructure. In particular, the extent to which infrastructure is likely to be undersupplied by private firms largely accounts for the degree of responsibility that government will assume for it. For example, some infrastructure projects, such as roads and water systems, display pronounced economies of scale; that is, they have high up-front (or fixed) costs to build and low incremental (or marginal) costs to operate and maintain, making it economically feasible for only one entity to undertake them (commonly referred to as a "natural monopoly"). Such projects may require public ownership—or at least public oversight—in order to maintain the price and supply of those infrastructure services at or near an economically efficient level (basically a level that is no higher than what is required to cover the cost of supplying the services). By contrast, a private firm in such a position would be expected to try to maximize profits by restricting supply and raising prices.

Another likely scenario for public-sector ownership arises when a private entity is not able to charge all users of the infrastructure a fee that is based on the value of the services they receive. Dams and other natural resource projects, for example, can provide various services, such as flood control and recreation, to a diffuse group of consumers. Because it is unclear who should be charged— and how much—for those services, they are referred to as public benefits.[5] Infrastructure whose public benefits are pronounced can be undersupplied by the private sector because it is harder for that sector to charge users enough to cover costs. Government can remedy that by supplying such services and recouping the cost through taxation.

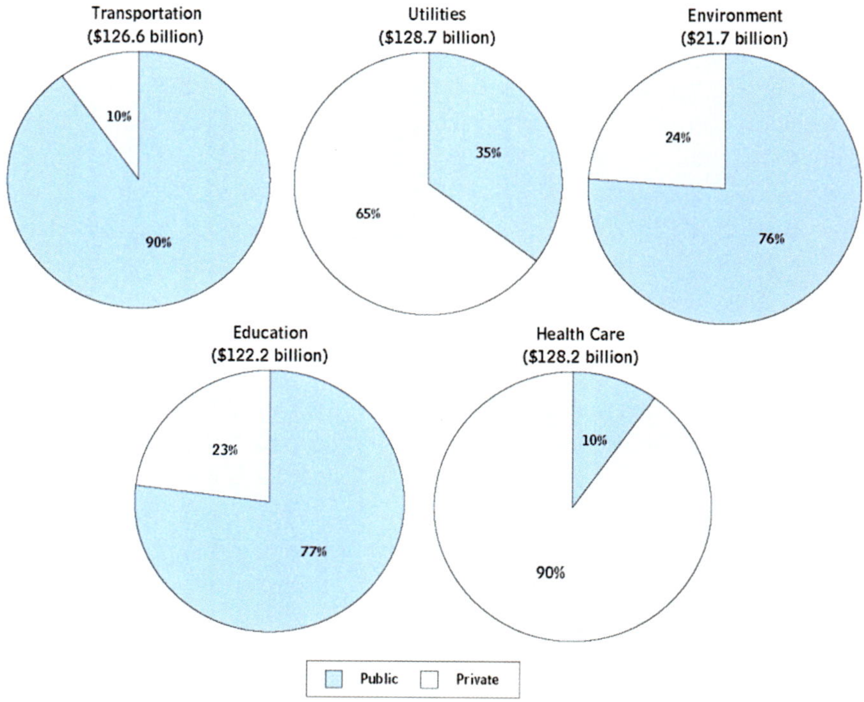

Source: Congressional Budget Office based on data and definitions of infrastructure categories in Table 1-1 of this report.

Note: Total capital spending by the public and private sectors in 2007 totaled $527.4 billion. The amounts in parentheses reflect the total capital spending on that type of infrastructure in 2007.

Figure 1.1. Total Capital Spending on Infrastructure in 2007, by Type of Infrastructure

Infrastructure that is less subject to scale economies or constraints on recouping costs—for instance, hospitals, postsecondary educational institutions, and pollution control and waste-disposal facilities—may be more suitable for private ownership. Even when infrastructure is privately owned, however, governments regularly provide financial support, oversight, or both. In addition, governments may offer tax benefits and make transfer payments to enable lower-income individuals to use that infrastructure. Such measures can provide an indirect source of public funding for investment in infrastructure that is primarily supplied by the private sector.

Capital Spending by Federal, State, and Local Governments

In 2007, the most recent year for which comprehensive data are available, federal spending on infrastructure totaled $68 billion, or about one-eighth of all capital expenditures on infrastructure in the United States. However, for specific types of projects—for example, transportation and environmental facilities—those outlays represent about one-half or more of the total investment.

Although public funding for infrastructure comes from all levels of government, state and local governments effectively have operational control over how the money will be spent. For example, about 80 percent of all federal capital spending on infrastructure, as defined in this study, is in the form of grants and loan subsidies to state and local governments (which must comply with some federally imposed conditions in order to receive those federal dollars).

Capital spending by states and localities out of their own tax receipts is also an important source of funding for infrastructure for which the public sector is the primary source of investment, especially transportation and water projects. States and localities have accounted for around 60 percent of total public capital spending on such projects over the past several decades (that measure does not include the federal government's contribution through tax preferences on municipal bonds).[6] State and local governments have been particularly important sources of investment in water and sewer infrastructure, supplying well over 90 percent of the $35 billion of public capital spending on those facilities in 2007 (see Figure 1-1).[7] They also have provided virtually all public investment in education facilities. Total state and local spending on infrastructure amounted to $215 billion in 2007.

Infrastructure projects undertaken by state and local governments are typically financed with tax-preferred bonds, which are then repaid with general tax receipts or revenues collected from users of the infrastructure. In some cases, private-sector investment in infrastructure may be eligible for tax-preferred financing, and state and local governments have historically controlled the decision as to whether to provide financing for private activities within their jurisdiction.[8]

Tax Preferences for Financing Infrastructure

For fiscal years 2008 to 2012, federal revenues forgone through the tax-exempt bond financing of infrastructure—both for new investments and for the refinancing of existing debt—are estimated to exceed $26 billion annually. Offering a federal tax preference for debt financing is one way of using the tax system to allocate economic resources. Like grants and loan subsidies, which are the alternative means of providing federal financial support to lower levels of government and the private sector, tax preferences may redirect federal revenues to state and local borrowers and, in some cases, reallocate resources from federal taxpayers to private entities. Tax preferences for debt financing therefore have consequences for both budgetary practice and economic efficiency.

Budgetary Implications

Federal tax preferences for municipal debt make the government's allocation of federal dollars less transparent and, because those preferences are outside the annual appropriation process, also limit the control the government exercises over that allocation. Four factors account for those effects: First, because the revenues forgone from tax preferences—which are known as **tax expenditures**— do not count as federal spending in calculating the budget, their widespread use masks the full scope of the government's activities.[9] Second, federal tax preferences potentially redistribute national income to constituents in the states and localities that make especially heavy use of them; in contrast to federal grants and loan subsidies, however, the amounts by which individual states benefit from tax preferences are not reported in the budget.[10] Third, because estimates of tax expenditures from the most common type of tax-preferred debt (that is, tax- exempt bonds issued by states and localities for their own purposes) are made annually at only an aggregate level, it is unclear how much any particular type of municipal project (say, spending on highways versus water utilities) benefits from tax preferences in a given year. As a consequence, the value of federal subsidies delivered through the tax system cannot always be compared with contemporaneous federal outlays in the same spending categories. Finally, under current federal budgetary practice, the federal government's control over the subsidy provided through tax preferences is limited because the amount of tax expenditures is not decided through the annual appropriation process—as is, for example, spending on infrastructure and other discretionary programs. Thus, tax expenditures constitute a form of "entitlement" spending whose amount is largely determined by circumstances outside the federal government's control.[11]

Tax expenditures offer some advantages over direct spending as a means of providing federal financial support. Tax preferences on municipal debt generally leave to states and localities the decision about which projects to finance and how much debt to issue. Issuers of those bonds are responsible for repaying the debt and may therefore be more prudent in how they allocate both their own funds and the federally subsidized portion of that spending than if they had simply received a federal grant. Moreover, although a federal financial subsidy could be delivered to borrowers through alternate means that would allow the subsidy to appear as spending on the budget—say, by making payments directly to those who report having provided financing for projects eligible for federal support—the current method of tax exemption and the claiming of tax credits are established means of delivering the same type of financial support to state and local governments.[12]

Economic Efficiency

Federal tax preferences for interest income from debt issued by states and localities make some investments more attractive than others and, as a result, redistribute some of the savings available for investment in the national economy to the governmental entities and private concerns that benefit from tax-preferred debt. A basic issue for policymakers as they consider establishing or setting the value of tax preferences is whether those subsidies stimulate investment that benefits the economy—and thus increases economic activity—and would otherwise have been underprovided because the states, localities, and private entities undertaking it would not have recouped enough of the total economic payoff.

Federal tax preferences may or may not be an economically efficient means of financing infrastructure projects. For example, offering a tax preference for financing a project undertaken by a particular state or locality could be economically efficient for the federal government if that investment was expected to generate economic benefits for taxpayers both nationwide and locally. (For economic efficiency, those who benefit from a project should bear its expense. Otherwise, too large a project might be undertaken—or too many infrastructure services might be consumed—relative to the resource cost of providing the project or services.) Offering a federal subsidy for the financing of infrastructure that provided only local benefits would thus not be an economically efficient use of federal revenues (it could, however, be rationalized on equity grounds, in that it could help ensure that all citizens had access to that type of facility).

Concerns about economic efficiency are particularly acute for the federal tax preferences that help finance private-sector investment in infrastructure, because those preferences risk transferring resources from taxpayers to private investors without obtaining a commensurate payoff in terms of the value of the infrastructure services that would not have been provided without that subsidy. For example, the fact that those infrastructure facilities are in private hands indicates that owners can capture— through user fees and other charges—a sizable portion of the value of the services they provide. Hence, public benefits from those investments may be small relative to those of infrastructure owned and operated by government, and determining the appropriate degree of subsidy—or whether any is warranted—may be difficult. If the private-sector investment would have taken place even without a subsidy, then the tax preference simply shifts resources from taxpayers to private investors. Because tax preferences for private-sector borrowers lower the cost of financing and hence the return needed to make an investment attractive, they can also reallocate capital from profitable projects to projects that otherwise would not have been undertaken, thereby potentially reducing economic growth.[13]

2. Tax-Preferred Bonds under Current Law

Like other activities carried out and paid for by state and local governments, infrastructure projects are eligible for financing with the proceeds of tax-preferred bonds. In some cases, federal tax preferences may also apply to the debt those governments issue to finance infrastructure (and other) activities undertaken primarily by the private sector.

The amount of tax-preferred debt issued to finance new infrastructure projects undertaken by the public and private sectors totaled almost $1.7 trillion from 1991 to 2007. About three-quarters of those bond proceeds, or roughly $1.3 trillion, was for capital spending on infrastructure by states and localities, and the remainder was used to fund private capital investment for projects that serve a public purpose, such as schools and hospitals. That $1.3 trillion amounted to over one-half of the $2.3 trillion in capital spending on infrastructure by state and local governments (that is, net of federal grants and loan subsidies). Since 1991, tax-exempt bonds have become a more important source of financing, particularly for public investment in transportation facilities, such as highways, and private investment in education.

That history and the projected demand for investment in the nation's infrastructure argue strongly for making federal subsidies for that capital spending as effective as possible. Understanding the advantages and disadvantages of the various types of tax preferences is therefore an important consideration for federal infrastructure policy.

The Internal Revenue Code provides for three forms of tax-preferred state and local bonds:

- **Tax-exempt bonds** pay interest to the bondholder that is not subject to federal income tax.
- **Tax-credit bonds,** by contrast, generally provide a credit against the bondholder's overall federal income tax liability.
- **Direct-pay tax-credit bonds,** in effect, require the federal government to make cash payments to the *issuer* of the bond in an amount equal to a portion of each of the interest payments the issuer makes to the bondholder.

Those tax preferences, and the spending measures by which the federal government supports investment in infrastructure, are shown in Figure 2-1.

Tax-Exempt Bonds

Tax-exempt bonds are the most well established type of tax-preferred debt (tax exemption dates to the beginning of the federal income tax in 1913) and are issued to finance either the general functions of state and local governments or certain projects undertaken by the private sector. Tax-exempt bonds reduce the issuer's borrowing costs because they normally can be sold at a lower rate of interest than can taxable debt of comparable risk and maturity.

Tax-exempt bonds must be issued by or on behalf of "qualified governmental units," which include a state or local government or any political subdivision thereof.[14] If bonds are issued directly by a state, city, or county, compliance with that requirement is easily determined; however, many bonds are issued by other entities that are not clearly political subdivisions of a state. In general, an entity is a political subdivision (and thereby a qualified governmental unit) only if it has more than an insubstantial amount of one or more of the following powers: taxation, eminent domain (that is, the ability to seize private property without the owner's consent—but with compensation), and law enforcement.[15]

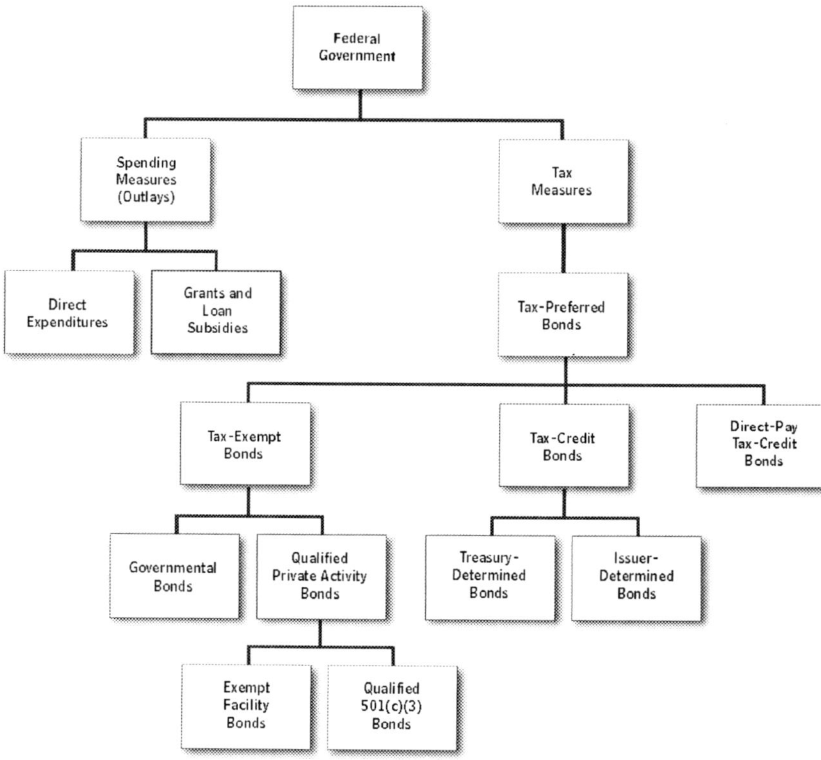

Sources: Congressional Budget Office and Joint Committee on Taxation.

Figure 2.1. How the Federal Government Finances Infrastructure

Tax-exempt bonds may be classified as either governmental bonds or private activity bonds. **Governmental bonds** are primarily used to finance governmental functions or are repaid with governmental funds. **Private activity bonds** provide financing to nongovernmental entities (for example, private businesses or individuals); a qualified governmental unit serves as a conduit between those entities and the purchaser of the bond. The tax exemption for interest on state and local bonds does not apply to private activity bonds unless those bonds are issued for certain permitted purposes and meet other requirements under the Internal Revenue Code. Bonds that meet such criteria are known as **qualified private activity bonds** and may be issued to finance a wide range of infrastructure projects.[16]

Governmental Bonds

Whether a bond is a governmental bond is determined by how its proceeds are used and how they are paid and secured, not by the type of facility being financed. Thus, a qualified governmental unit may issue governmental bonds to finance general government operations and services, including physical infrastructure such as transportation, utilities, environmental projects, schools, and hospitals.[17] However, although the types of projects eligible for governmental bond financing are not circumscribed, current law imposes restrictions on the parties that may benefit from such financing. For example, current law limits the amount of proceeds from governmental bonds that nongovernmental entities can use; if that amount exceeds the limit, those bonds may be treated as private activity bonds rather than as governmental bonds. Only certain types of private activity bonds—known as qualified private activity bonds and discussed in detail below—are tax-exempt.

Private Activity Bonds

Generally, private activity bonds—only some of which are tax-exempt—are defined by the Code as any bond that satisfies either of two criteria: (1) the private *business use* test and the private *security or payment* test (jointly referred to as the private business test); or (2) the private loan financing test.[18]

Under the **private business test,** a bond is a private activity bond if it is part of an issue in which:

- More than 10 percent of the proceeds of the issue (including use of the bond-financed property) is to be used in the trade or business of any person other than a governmental unit ("private *business use* test"), as specified in sec. 141(b) (1); and
- More than 10 percent of the payment of principal or interest on the issue is, directly or indirectly, secured by (a) property used or to be used for a private business use (or payments in respect of such property) or (b) to be derived from payments in respect of property, or borrowed money, used or to be used for a private business use ("*private security or payment* test"), as specified in sec. 141(b) (2).

The two prongs of the private business test are conjunctive; that is, a bond is a private activity bond only if both conditions are met. Thus, the bonds financing a facility that is 100 percent privately used are not private activity bonds if they are not secured by or repaid with private payments. For example, a city may use governmental bonds to finance the relocation of privately owned utility lines if the bonds will be paid from tax assessments rather than from payments by the utility or its ratepayers.[19]

A bond issue also will be treated as a private activity bond if the issue satisfies the **private loan financing test**, that is, if proceeds exceeding the lesser of $5 million or 5 percent of the issue are used directly or indirectly to finance loans to one or more nongovernmental persons (sec. 141(c)).[20]

Qualified Private Activity Bonds Issued to Finance Infrastructure Investment

The interest income on some private activity bonds may be eligible for tax-exempt status, thus allowing tax-exempt financing to be provided for certain private activities through what are known as **qualified private activity bonds**.[21] A qualified governmental unit generally acts as the "conduit issuer" of the debt, and the "conduit borrower" is the nongovernmental entity that receives the benefit of tax-exempt financing for those bonds. Two types of qualified private activity bonds are used to finance infrastructure: exempt facility bonds and qualified 501(c) (3) bonds.

To qualify as an **exempt facility bond**, at least 95 percent of the bond's net proceeds must be used to finance an eligible facility (sec. 142). Infrastructure facilities eligible for that financing include transportation (airports, docks and wharves, local mass commuting, high-speed intercity rail facilities, and qualified highway or surface freight transfer facilities); privately owned or operated public works facilities (water, sewage, solid and hazardous waste disposal, and local district heating or cooling facilities); certain private facilities that provide electricity or gas locally; and qualified public educational facilities.

Qualified 501 (c)(3) bonds may be used to finance the activities of infrastructure projects by organizations described in sec. 501(c) (3) of the Code and exempt from federal income tax under sec. 501(c).[22] Those organizations are permitted to finance their exempt activities, such as charitable endeavors or efforts to promote social welfare, on a tax-exempt basis. Infrastructure projects undertaken by sec. 501(c) (3) organizations that are eligible for such financing include schools and hospitals.

Investment that falls outside this study's definition of infrastructure may also be financed by qualified private activity bonds. Examples include qualified mortgages, residential rental properties, student loans, and a few other activities.

Restrictions on Qualified Private Activity Bonds

Generally, qualified private activity bonds are subject to restrictions that do not apply to governmental bonds. For example, many types of qualified private activity bonds are subject to an annual cap on the aggregate volume that can be issued. One such limit—referred to as the **unified volume cap** because it applies to the combined issuance of the different types of qualified private activity bonds subject to it—is imposed at the state level.[23] For calendar year 2009, those annual volume limits, which are indexed for inflation, equal the greater of $90 per state resident or $273.27 million.[24]

Some qualified private activity bonds are not subject to the unified volume cap. Such bonds include those that finance infrastructure projects such as airports, docks, and wharves; nonprofit activities undertaken by qualified 501 (c)(3) organizations such as education and health care facilities; and certain facilities if they are government owned (for example, high-speed intercity rail and solid waste disposal). In addition, bonds that are subject to separate local, state, or national volume caps are not subject to the unified volume cap. Examples of such bonds issued to finance infrastructure investment include qualified public education facility bonds and qualified highway or surface freight transfer facility bonds.

If the aggregate amount of qualified private activity bonds issued in a particular state during a calendar year is less than the volume cap, the authority may elect to allow all (or any portion) of the difference to be carried forward to subsequent years for one or more of four purposes specified in the Code:

- Issuing exempt facility bonds;
- Issuing qualified mortgage bonds or mortgage credit certificates;
- Issuing qualified student loan bonds; and
- Issuing qualified redevelopment bonds.

Carryforwards of an unused volume cap are valid for three years.

Qualified private activity bonds also are subject to limitations on the costs of issuing the bond, its maturity, and federal tax liability. The costs of issuing the bond (for example, legal and underwriting fees) that may be paid from the proceeds of qualified private activity bonds are generally limited to 2 percent per bond. Most qualified private activity bonds are subject to a term-to-maturity rule that limits the period of time such bonds may remain outstanding. Generally, that rule provides that the average maturity of a qualified private activity bond cannot exceed 120 percent of the economic life of the property being financed.[25] In addition, the interest income from qualified private activity bonds (other than qualified 501(c) (3) bonds issued after August 7, 1986) is generally subject to the alternative minimum tax (sec. 57(a) (5)), although the AMT does not apply to private activity bonds issued during 2009 and 2010 (see sec. 57(a)(5)(C)(vi).[26]

Tax-Credit Bonds

In contrast to tax-exempt bonds, tax-credit bonds are much more recent in origin (however, the Congress's interest in them spans a number of decades—see Box 2-1). The first tax-credit bonds were added to the Internal Revenue Code in 1997, effective for 1998. Although the outstanding amount of tax-credit bonds currently is minuscule in comparison with that of tax- exempt bonds, tax-credit bonds have two features that would in theory enable federal subsidies for borrowing to be delivered more efficiently:

- They can be more cost-effective, and
- The amount of the tax credit can be adjusted.

Tax-credit bonds can be more cost-effective than tax-exempt bonds because every dollar of federal revenue forgone through the tax credit is transferred to borrowers, whereas only a portion of the federal revenue forgone through a tax exemption lowers financing costs for bond issuers. Second, although tax-credit bonds have tended to provide a subsidy that is close to 100 percent of interest costs, the amount of the tax credit can be adjusted, depending on the purpose for which the bonds are issued. By adjusting the credit amount, the Congress effectively can exempt more or less of each dollar of interest income on a bond and tailor the federal subsidy to the public benefit the Congress expects to derive from the project being subsidized.

Tax-credit bonds subsidize the issuer's cost of borrowing by providing a tax credit in lieu of (or in addition to) the payment of interest to the holder of the bond or, in some cases, directly to the issuer. Tax-credit bonds can be divided into two categories:

- **Treasury-determined** (for which the credit rate is set by the Secretary of the Treasury), and

- **Issuer-determined** (for which the credit is calculated on the basis of an interest rate set by the issuer).

The first Treasury-determined tax-credit bonds, known as Qualified Zone Academy Bonds, were added to the Code in 1997, and seven others have since been added. The first issuer-determined tax-credit bonds, known as Build America Bonds, were added to the Code in 2009.

Treasury-Determined Bonds

The eight types of Treasury-determined tax-credit bonds and the sections of the Code that authorize them (given in parentheses) are as follows: Qualified Zone Academy Bonds (sec. 54E), Gulf Tax-Credit Bonds (sec. 1400N(1) (4)), Midwest Tax-Credit Bonds,[27] Qualified Energy Conservation Bonds (sec. 54D), Clean Renewable Energy Bonds (sec. 54),[28] New Clean Renewable Energy Bonds (sec. 54C), Qualified Forestry Conservation Bonds (sec. 54B), and Qualified School Construction Bonds (sec. 54F). Each type of Treasury- determined tax-credit bond is subject to certain special rules and volume limitations, the discussion of which goes beyond the scope of this paper.[29]

2.1. History of Congressional Proposals for Alternatives to Tax Exemption for Municipal Bonds

For more than 40 years, Members of Congress have been proposing various alternatives to tax exemption as a means of subsidizing state and local borrowing. Two such alternatives are payments the federal government would make directly to the issuers of municipal bonds and a tax credit equal to a percentage of the taxable interest paid on bonds.

Direct Payment

Several proposals for a direct subsidy date back to 1968. In that year, Senator William Proxmire proposed extending a federal guarantee to the debt of state and local bond issuers who elected to receive the guarantee; interest on the bonds covered by the guarantee would have been taxable, and the federal government would have paid issuers amounts equal to one-third of each interest payment on the bonds.[1]

In 1969, Congressmen Wilbur Mills and John Byrnes introduced a similar bill that would have allowed state and local entities to issue taxable bonds and receive payments from the federal government equal to a percentage (fixed at the time of issuance at between 25 percent and 40 percent) of the interest paid on the bonds. The Secretary of the Treasury would have adjusted that percentage on a quarterly basis to reflect the amount determined to be "necessary for the United States to pay in order to encourage the States and political subdivisions thereof to make [the election]."[2] The provision was included in H.R. 13270, the Tax Reform Act of 1969, as passed by the House of Representatives, but was not part of the Senate bill or the Conference Agreement.[3]

In 1973, Senator Edmund S. Muskie proposed making direct payments to state and local entities that issued taxable bonds. Those payments would have been equal to 50 percent of the interest, the highest level in any proposed bill.[4]

A novel proposal for a direct subsidy by Senator Pete V. Domenici in 1983 would have tied the amount of the federal subsidy to the spread between the yields on state and local bonds and Treasury bonds. Senator Domenici's bill would have permitted municipalities to issue taxable bonds and then would have required the federal government to make direct payments to the issuers equal to a percentage of the interest paid on the bonds. That percentage was determined by taking 100 percent and then reducing it by a percentage that was calculated by taking the interest yield of Moody's AAA-rated tax-exempt bonds and dividing that yield by the interest yield for the most recent Treasury bond of like maturity.[5] As the yield on Treasury bonds relative to tax-exempt municipal bonds rose, the subsidy also would have increased. Although the proposal in some sense tied the subsidy to the value the market placed on the tax exemption, it ignored the other factors—such as an increase in the perceived credit risk of debt issued by state and local governments relative to obligations of the federal government—that might drive down the yield on Treasury bonds relative to the yields on municipal bonds.

Tax Credit

The first bill providing for a credit rather than a direct payment or exemption was introduced in 1974 by Senator William D. Hathaway. That bill would have given the holders of the tax-credit bonds a credit equal to 30 percent of the taxable interest paid on the bonds.[6] Five years later, Senator John C. Danforth proposed an even more generous credit—67 percent—for any person who chose to include the interest payable on formerly exempt municipal bonds.[7]

[1] S. 3170, 90th Cong. (1968).
[2] H.R. 13270, 91st Cong., sec. 602(b) (1969).
[3] Id.
[4] S. 1439, 93d Cong., sec. 502(b) (1973). In 1978, the Carter Administration proposed a taxable bond election for state and local issuers that would have been coupled with a subsidy equal to 30 percent of the interest payments. See *Budget of the United States Government, Fiscal Year 1978: Budget Receipts* (H. Doc. 9 5-28, Vol. IX), at 62.
[5] S. 533, 98th Cong., sec. 103(a)(2) (1983).
[6] S. 4124, 93d Cong., sec. 42(a) (1974).
[7] S. 1021, 96th Cong., sec. 44D(a) (1979).

In general, a taxpayer holding a Treasury-determined tax-credit bond at specific times during the year (typically referred to as credit allowance dates) is entitled to a tax credit. The amount of the credit is determined by multiplying the bond's credit rate by the face amount of the holder's bond. The credit rate for the bonds, as determined by the Secretary of the Treasury, is the rate (or a percentage of the rate) that permits the qualified tax- credit bond to be issued without a discount and without interest cost to the qualified issuer (the "clearing rate").[30] The credit for Treasury-determined tax-credit bonds is 100 percent of the clearing rate, with two exceptions: For Qualified Energy Conservation Bonds (QECs) and New Clean Renewable Energy Bonds (New CREBs), the credit rate is 70 percent of the clearing rate. The credit accrues quarterly and is included in the bondholder's gross income as if it were an interest payment on the bond; it can be claimed against liability under the regular income tax and the alternative minimum tax. Unused credits may be carried forward to succeeding tax years. In addition, for certain types of tax-credit bonds (known as **qualified tax-credit bonds**), credits may be separated from the ownership of the underlying bond similar to the way in which interest coupons can be stripped from interest-bearing bonds in order to separate payment of principal from payment of interest.[31]

Issuer-Determined Bonds

The American Recovery and Reinvestment Act of 2009 created Build America Bonds, a new type of tax-credit bond that supplements interest paid by the issuer with a fixed-rate tax credit to the holder of the bond. The bondholder must report both the interest payment and the credit as taxable income. Build America Bonds may be issued only in 2009 and 2010. An issuer of those bonds elects to have an otherwise tax-exempt bond treated as a **taxable**

governmental bond, that is, as any obligation (other than a private activity bond) if the interest on it would otherwise be excludable from gross income under sec. 103 and if the issuer makes an irrevocable election to have the provision apply.

Unlike the credit for Treasury-determined tax-credit bonds, the credit rate on Build America Bonds is set by law at 35 percent of the interest, or coupon, payment the bondholder receives from the issuer. (Presumably, the interest rate is a market rate that varies with the issuer's creditworthiness, the bond's maturity date, and other factors that typically determine a borrower's cost of funds.) The holder of a Build America Bond generally receives a tax credit of 35 percent of the interest paid on the bond on each of the due dates during the calendar year (original issue discount is not treated as a payment of interest for purposes of determining the credit).[32] The sum of the accrued credits is allowed against the regular income tax and the alternative minimum tax. Any unused portion of the credit may be carried forward to succeeding taxable years. The credit and the interest paid by the issuer are included in gross income; the credit may be stripped under rules similar to those provided in sec. 54A regarding qualified tax-credit bonds.

Build America Bonds should sell at the same price as comparable taxable bonds; because of the 35 percent tax credit, however, the interest paid by the issuer of the bond will be considerably smaller—approximately 74.1 percent of the amount due on a taxable bond. Consider, for example, two bonds—a taxable bond and a Build America Bond—that have a face value of $1,000 (the amount due at maturity). The taxable bond sells at par (at its face value) and has a $60 coupon (that is, it pays 6 percent in interest). The Build America Bond, which has a coupon of $44.40—that is, it pays 4.4 percent in interest (74.1 percent of 6 percent)—should also sell at par. The taxpayer who acquires the Build America Bond will receive an interest payment of $44.40 and may claim a credit of $15.60 (35 percent of $44.40). The credit and the interest payment are both included in the taxpayer's income. Thus, his or her taxable income from the bond would be $60 ($44.40 plus $15.60)—the same amount that would accrue to the holder of a comparable taxable bond.

Direct-Pay Tax-Credit Bonds

As part of the authorization of Build America Bonds, the American Recovery and Reinvestment Act created several issuer-determined, direct-pay tax-credit bonds. Such bonds—known as qualified Build America Bonds—

must be sold in 2009 or 2010; in addition, 100 percent of the proceeds from them (net of a "reasonable" amount of proceeds set aside as reserves for future bond payments) must be used for capital expenditures. However, in lieu of a tax credit going to the bondholder, a credit equal to 35 percent of each interest payment (excluding any original issue discount) can be claimed by the issuer. The issuer does not pay tax on that credit and therefore pays less interest than for other types of Build America Bonds. For example, the issuer of a direct-pay Build America Bond in the scenario above (in which the taxable bond has a face value of $1,000 and a coupon of 6 percent) receives a payment of $21 for each $60 coupon paid to bondholders (35 percent of $60). Because the issuer does not pay tax on the payment, its net interest cost is $39, compared with $44.40 if the bondholder claimed the credit instead.[33]

3. Issuance of Tax-Preferred Bonds and Investment in Infrastructure, 1991 to 2007

Tax-preferred bonds can be issued to finance capital spending on infrastructure by either state and local governments or the private sector. Until recently, such debt has almost exclusively taken the form of tax-exempt bonds, with tax-credit bonds playing only a very small role. The importance of tax-exempt bonds as a means of financing investment has not changed much for infrastructure as a whole; it has risen slightly for capital spending by state and local governments and has fallen for investment by the private sector. Tax-exempt bonds have, however, played an increasing role in financing transportation projects undertaken by state and local governments and private investment in education.

Trends in the Issuance of Tax-Preferred Bonds

The amount of tax-preferred debt issued to finance new infrastructure projects undertaken by state and local governments and the private sector totaled almost $1.7 trillion from 1991 to 2007. That amount does not reflect issuance of tax-credit bonds (which are a relatively insignificant source of financing) and does not include proceeds of tax-exempt bonds whose issuance is not reported in an infrastructure category but could nonetheless have financed infrastructure projects.

Trends in the amount of tax-preferred debt issued to finance infrastructure investment are based on data published by the Internal Revenue Service (IRS). Those data are sufficiently detailed to allow the amount of tax- exempt debt issued for projects within infrastructure categories to be tracked on an annual basis. In contrast, relatively little information is available on the issuance of tax-credit bonds, and this chapter considers them only briefly. Unless otherwise indicated, all references to tax-exempt bonds refer to bonds issued to finance new infrastructure projects; such bonds are known as **new-money** issues. In contrast, tax-exempt bonds that refinance debt incurred in the past are known as **refunding issues.**[34]

Inferences about the amount of tax-exempt bond proceeds going to infrastructure are subject to several qualifications. In particular, the use of tax-exempt bonds to finance investment in infrastructure is understated to the extent that bond proceeds that are not reported in any of the infrastructure categories identified in this study are in fact spent on infrastructure. For example, a single municipal bond may be issued to finance diverse projects, because bundling that financing into one bond is cheaper than issuing separate bonds for each activity. As a result, 30 percent of the proceeds from governmental bonds issued during the 1991–2007 period—including bonds issued to finance infrastructure as well as other activities—were reported by their issuers as being for "other purposes," which means either that the specific purpose(s) listed on the reporting form did not apply or that the issuer did not allocate the bonds' proceeds among separate purposes. Such bonds could have financed new investment in infrastructure along with other activities; that possibility is particularly relevant to education because states often issue bonds whose proceeds are used to finance construction of education facilities and for other purposes. In contrast, the opposite scenario—in which the issuance of tax-exempt education bonds financed both capital spending on infrastructure and activities unrelated to infrastructure investment (such as student loan programs)—appears less significant (see Box 3-1).

The system that the IRS uses to classify the purpose for which qualified private activity bonds are issued is more precise than the one it uses for governmental obligations. As a result, the issuance of such bonds can be classified by type of infrastructure project more completely than that of governmental bonds, and the amount of proceeds classified in the "other purposes" category is never more than a few tenths of a percent in any year from 1991 through 2007.[35]

One exception, however, is a type of qualified private activity bond—a nonhospital 501(c)(3) bond—that can be used to finance a variety of nonprofit activities related to infrastructure. The share of those bonds in the overall issuance of new-money qualified private activity bonds has increased sharply since the early 1990s, rising from a level of 20 percent during the early to mid-1990s to a high of almost 40 percent in the 2000–2003 period before settling back to around 30 percent by 2007. This study allocates the annual proceeds of those bonds to specific infrastructure categories (namely "education" and "health care") on the basis of the results of an unpublished IRS analysis. As with governmental bonds, however, a large share (over 30 percent) of the proceeds of nonhospital 501(c) (3) bonds cannot be attributed to any type of project, and so the importance of that source of financing to infrastructure is probably also understated.

Finally, not all of the proceeds from tax-exempt bonds are actually spent to finance the infrastructure projects for which they are issued. Some of the proceeds from a bond sale may also be used to cover the costs associated with the debt-financing process itself (for example, expenses to issue bonds, to obtain bond insurance and other forms of credit enhancement, and to create a reserve fund in case projected sources of repayment funds fall short). As a result, the data on tax-exempt bonds used in this analysis generally include a very small amount of proceeds—about 2 percent—that is not invested in infrastructure.[36]

Tax-Exempt Bonds

Because of volume caps and other restrictions on qualified private activity bonds, governmental bonds—whose issuance is not subject to such constraints—provide the bulk of tax-exempt financing for new investments in infrastructure. Governmental bonds accounted for about three-quarters ($1.3 trillion) of the $1.7 trillion in tax-exempt debt issued to finance new investment in infrastructure from 1991 to 2007, compared with $372 billion for qualified private activity bonds.[37]

The amount of tax-exempt debt issued has increased significantly—and, for governmental bonds, fairly regularly—since the mid-1990s (see Figure 3-1). At least two factors have probably contributed to that increase: First, the demand for greater investment in infrastructure boosted the demand for debt financing. Second, the steady decline in interest rates charged to municipal borrowers during that period made it cheaper for them to finance any amount of capital spending by issuing debt.

The jump in the issuance of governmental bonds in 2006 and 2007 was mainly due to sharp increases in the sale of such bonds to finance new investment in utilities, education, and transportation.

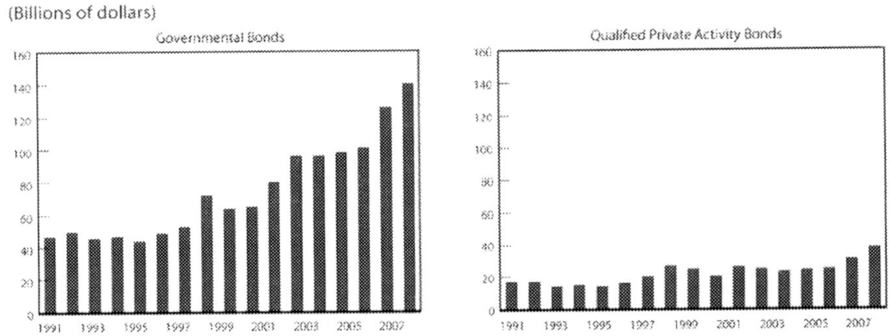

Source: Congressional Budget Office based on data from the Internal Revenue Service.

Figure 3.1. Issuance of Tax-Exempt Bonds for New Investment in Infrastructure, Calendar Years 1991 to 2007

Governmental Bonds

Whether measured in the aggregate over the 1991–2007 period or on an annual basis, education bonds have accounted for the largest share of governmental obligations issued to finance new investment in infrastructure (see Figure 3-2). Education bonds made up $620 billion, or 49 percent, of the $1.3 trillion of such bonds issued over the 1991–2007 period to finance that investment. Transportation and utilities accounted for $252 billion and $230 billion (20 percent and 18 percent), respectively; environmental projects (including sewage), for $131 billion (10 percent); and health care projects, for $42 billion (3 percent). Education also claims the largest share on a yearly basis, followed by bonds for transportation, utilities, and, through much of the 1 990s, environmental projects.[38] A notably smaller amount of governmental bonds has been issued annually to finance new capital spending on health care projects.

Qualified Private Activity Bonds

Compared with governmental bonds, qualified private activity bonds account for a smaller share of total financing for new investment in infrastructure (about one-quarter) and have a different allocation among infrastructure categories (see Figure 3-3 on page 21 and Box 3-2 on page 23). From 1991 to 2007, health care bonds accounted for $200 billion (53 percent) of the $372 billion of total issuance of qualified private activity bonds; transportation bonds, for $67 billion (18 percent); education bonds (primarily for colleges and universities), for $62 billion (17 percent); environmental projects (that is, solid and hazardous waste disposal), for $35 billion (9 percent); and utilities (including sewage, water supply, and energy), for $8 billion (2 percent). From year to year, bonds issued to finance health care projects (such as hospitals) also claimed the largest share of qualified private activity bond proceeds for infrastructure purposes, and issuance of education bonds posted the largest annual rate of growth (about 11 percent).[39]

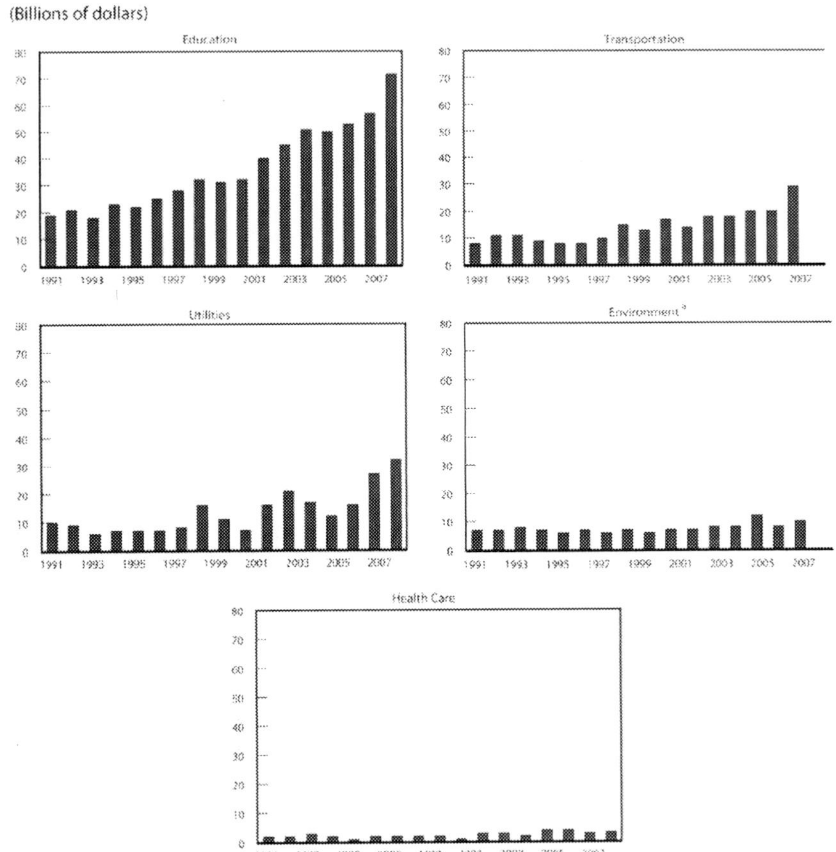

Source: Congressional Budget Office based on data from the Internal Revenue Service.

Note: Infrastructure categories come from the classification scheme on Internal Revenue Service Form 8038-G (Information Return for Tax-Exempt Governmental Obligations).

a. Includes sewage bonds.

Figure 3.2. Issuance of Governmental Bonds for New Investment, by Type of Infrastructure, Calendar Years 1991 to 2007

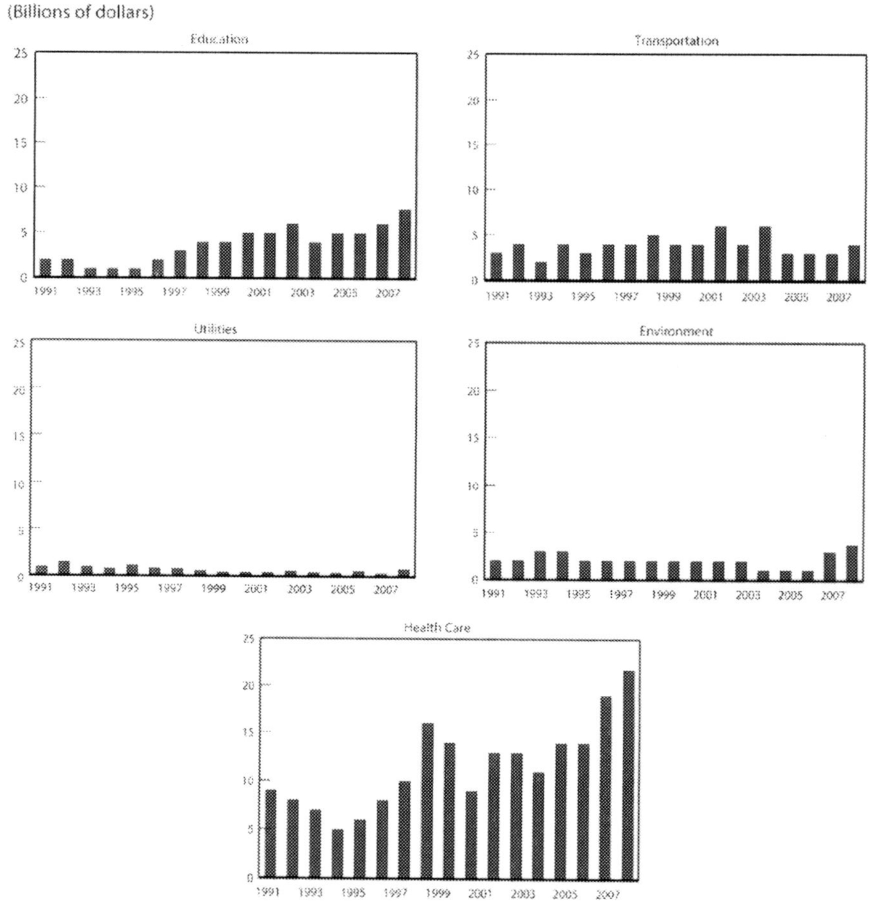

Source: Congressional Budget Office based on data from the Internal Revenue Service.

Note: Infrastructure categories reflect the grouping of qualified private activity bonds as identified on Internal Revenue Service Form 8038 (Information Return for Tax-Exempt Private Activity Bond Issues). See Box 3-2 for a description of those categories.

Figure 3.3. Issuance of Qualified Private Activity Bonds for New Investment, by Type of Infrastructure, Calendar Years 1991 to 2007

3.1. The Use of Education Bonds for Human Rather Than Physical Capital

The data on tax-exempt bonds issued for new investment in education reported in this study will overstate the amount of infrastructure financing to the extent that the proceeds of those bonds are used to finance student loan programs and other activities that contribute to the formation of intangible assets (for example, human capital) rather than physical capital (such as education facilities and equipment). According to Thomson Financial, the proceeds of bonds allocated to student loans accounted for approximately 13 percent of the annual value of municipal debt issued for educational purposes from 1991 to 2007.[1] That figure applies to the combined issuance of governmental bonds, qualified private activity bonds, and taxable bonds and covers bonds issued for new investment and for refinancing.

Evidence suggests that the sale of debt for educational purposes other than investment in structures and equipment does not weaken this study's findings for tax-exempt bond issuance and its importance for infrastructure financing. First, the proceeds of governmental bonds generally cannot be used to finance student loans because of the restriction on private-loan financing (sec. 141(c) of the Internal Revenue Code). Reflecting that fact, *The Bond Buyer Yearbook* reports that among the major sales of debt for educational purposes in 2007, most bonds issued to finance student loan programs were either taxable or subject to the alternative minimum tax (AMT).[2] Those AMT-liable bonds are probably qualified private activity bonds authorized by sec. 144(b) of the Code and, as such, are identified separately on Internal Revenue Service (IRS) Form 8038 and therefore can be excluded from this analysis. In addition, other types of qualified private activity bonds that may be issued to finance education generally and student loan programs in particular (for example, tax-exempt 501(c) (3) bonds authorized by sec. 145(a) of the Code) are also not likely to overstate the capital spending on education infrastructure reported in this study, because those data include only bonds issued by or on behalf of schools, and the proceeds of such bonds are typically used only for capital projects.

[1] See Thomson Financial, *The Bond Buyer Yearbook* (New York: SourceMedia, various years).

[2] See Thomson Financial, *The Bond Buyer Yearbook, 2008* (2008), pp. 140–141.

3.2. Types of Infrastructure Financed by Qualified Private Activity Bonds

The data on qualified private activity bonds presented in the text and in Figure 3-3 on page 21 follow the definitions based on Internal Revenue Service (IRS) Form 8038 (Information Return for Tax-Exempt Private Activity Bond Issues) and, in some cases, unpublished information from the IRS.

Education comprises "qualified section 501(c) (3) nonhospital" bonds; the proceeds of those bonds are allocated to "education" on the basis of unpublished data from the IRS. Qualified private activity bonds may also be issued to finance "qualified public education" facilities; however, their issuance is not reported separately by the IRS in some years to avoid disclosure of individual issues.

Transportation includes "airports" and "docks and wharves" facility bonds. Although qualified private activity bonds are also issued for "mass commuting" and "high-speed railway" facilities, the annual amount of that issuance is either less than $1 million (and hence reported as zero) or not reported separately by the IRS in order to avoid disclosure of individual issues.

Utilities include "local electricity or gas," "water supply," "sewage," and "local district heating or cooling" facility bonds.

Environment includes "solid waste disposal" and "qualified hazardous waste" facility bonds.

Health care includes "qualified hospital" (that is, 501(c) (3)) bonds and, on the basis of unpublished IRS data, proceeds from the issuance of some "qualified nonhospital" bonds for hospitals, clinics, and other health care projects.

The consistently large amount of health care bonds and the rapid growth in the issuance of education bonds (relative to that of other qualified private activity issues) may be due in part to the fact that nonprofits can finance their activities by issuing those bonds at tax-free rates of interest while earning returns from other assets in their portfolio at taxable rates (but they do not pay taxes on those returns). That practice, known as **tax arbitrage**, can provide an important financial benefit to such organizations, although the Internal Revenue Code attempts to limit that practice with regard to tax-exempt bonds.[40]

Tax-Credit Bonds

The issuance of tax-credit bonds to finance infrastructure projects has been limited. For example, a recent article analyzed the data available for Qualified Zone Academy Bonds (QZABs), which finance certain types of education facilities.[41] Those data were obtained from filings of the Internal Revenue Service's Form 8860 for 2005, which taxpayers (in this case, financial institutions such as banks and insurance companies) use to claim the QZAB credit. Approximately $2.1 billion in outstanding QZAB principal was reported to the IRS in 2005, which amounts to only about two-thirds of the total authorized to have been issued during that time. The other limited data that are available appear to confirm that, for other types of tax-credit bonds, issuances have been well below authorized amounts. For example, a recent article concluded that the amount of Clean Renewable Energy Bonds that has been issued is only a small fraction of the amount authorized.[42]

The Importance of Tax-Preferred Financing for Investment in Infrastructure

Reliance on tax-preferred bonds as a means of financing investment in infrastructure—roughly measured as the ratio of the cumulative amount of bonds issued for new investment relative to capital spending on infrastructure from 1991 to 2007—is more pronounced for state and local governments than for private businesses. The difference is consistent with two basic features of infrastructure spending financed by issuing qualified private activity bonds: Issuance is restricted to certain types of projects, and the amount of bonds sold in a given year may also be capped.

Although tax-exempt bonds serve as a means of financing investment in infrastructure, only a portion of that issuance—equal to the savings in financing costs conveyed through their tax-exempt status—can be considered a source of funding. Future payments on infrastructure debt typically will be made with tax receipts or with payments from users of the infrastructure services in question.[43] Taxpayers also must make up for the federal revenues forgone through the tax exemptions.

Assessing the role of tax-exempt bonds as a means of financing investment in infrastructure—and determining the trend in that relationship over time—is challenging. It requires matching the annual issuance of bonds to particular infrastructure spending categories and then distributing the proceeds of those bonds annually among the years required to complete the infrastructure project in question. However, the issuance of bonds and capital spending on infrastructure are not contemporaneous— bonds to finance infrastructure projects may be issued to investors up front, whereas infrastructure projects usually require several years to complete.

Table 3.1. Issuance of Governmental Bonds for New Investment and Capital Spending by State and Local Governments, by Type of Infrastructure, 1991 to 2007

	Governmental Bonds[a]		Capital Spending by the Public Sector[b]		Governmental Bonds as a Share of Capital Spending (Percent)	Annualized Rate of Growth		
	Amount (Billions of dollars)	Share of Total (Percent)	Amount (Billions of dollars)	Share of Total (Percent)		Governmental Bonds (Percent)	Total Capital Spending (Percent)	Difference (Percentage points)
Education	619.9	49	956.2	42	65	8.5	7.8	0.7
Transportation	251.8	20	715.3	31	35	7.3	5.1	2.2
Utilities	229.6	18	262.5	12	87	7.6	5.2	2.3
Environment[c]	131.1	10	242.1	11	54	1.6	5.7	-4.1
Health Care	42.3	3	104.6	5	40	2.7	5.5	-2.7
Total	**1,274.8**	**100**	**2,280.7**	**100**	**n.a.**	**7.1**	**6.3**	**0.9**

Source: Congressional Budget Office.

Note: n.a. = not applicable.

a. Calendar year data.

b. Fiscal year data, net of federal grants and loan subsidies. Capital spending in 2007 has been estimated.

c. Includes sewage bonds.

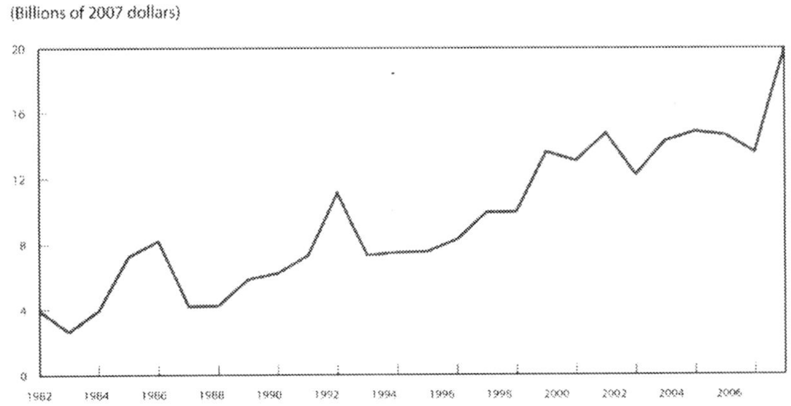

Source: Congressional Budget Office based on data from the Federal Highway Administration.

Figure 3.4. Proceeds from State Bonds Used for New Investment in Highways, 1982 to 2007

The Congressional Budget Office has also found that annual spending rates of federal grants for state and local investment may vary considerably by infrastructure category and by type of project within categories. As a result, it is difficult to accurately distribute on a yearly basis the proceeds from the issuance of municipal bonds. For that reason, in assessing the reliance of the public and private sectors on tax-exempt bond financing, this study simply compares the cumulative amounts of bonds issued and capital spending across the period for which data are available (1991–2007); to infer the trend in that relationship over time (either overall or for particular types of infrastructure), this study assumes that tax-exempt bonds have increased their importance as a means of financing investment in infrastructure if the growth in their annual issuance has exceeded the growth in capital spending over that period.[44]

Governmental Bonds

Over the 1991–2007 period, issuance of governmental bonds for new investment in infrastructure totaled $1.3 trillion, compared with $2.3 trillion of capital spending on infrastructure by state and local governments (net of federal grants and loan subsidies). The implied reliance of those governments on tax-exempt bonds to finance their capital spending varies by type of infrastructure: The ratio of governmental bond issuance to capital spending was highest for investment in utilities (87 percent), followed by education (65 percent) and the environment (54 percent).[45] In contrast, states and localities made less use of governmental bonds to finance investment in health care and transportation infrastructure. The ratios of bond proceeds to capital spending in those categories were 40 percent and 35 percent, respectively (see Table 3-1).

From 1991 to 2007, tax-exempt bonds were increasingly important as a means of financing state and local investment in transportation. The annual increase in the issuance of governmental bonds for that purpose was 7.3 percent, outpacing growth in capital spending on that infrastructure (5.1 percent) by more than 2 percentage points. Although issuance of governmental bonds for new investment in utilities also grew faster than capital spending (by 2.3 percentage points), that growth differential disappears when the calculation excludes 2006 and 2007 (years in which an especially large amount of utility bonds was issued—see Figure 3-2 on page 20). Annual issuance of governmental bonds for new investment in education from 1991 through 2007 grew faster than state and local capital spending by about 0.7 percentage points. However, that growth differential disappears when data for 2007 are excluded (sales of education bonds were exceptionally strong in that year). In contrast, growth in the annual issuance of governmental bonds for projects related to the environment and to health care was slower (by several percentage points) than the growth of capital spending by states and localities on that infrastructure.

Other sources also point to an increased role for bonds in financing investment in transportation projects—at least for investment in highways. The Government Accountability Office concluded that states' issuance of bonds for highways rose fairly steadily from 1982 to 2001—registering a 270 percent increase (in constant dollars) by the end of the period—and that state and local investment (net of federal grants and loan subsidies and adjusted for inflation) rose by 166 percent over the same period.[46] The importance of tax-exempt bond financing to highway investment leveled off after 2001 before rising sharply again in 2007 (see Figure 3-4, which shows the trend in state borrowing to finance new investment in highways). That trend is consistent with a spike in bond-financed capital spending on highways coming a year after a jump in issuance of new-money bonds for transportation (an increase of $9 billion from 2005 to 2006).[47]

Qualified Private Activity Bonds

Issuance of qualified private activity bonds for new investment in infrastructure from 1991 to 2007 totaled $372 billion (see Table 3-2). That amount accounts for roughly 13 percent of the $2.7 trillion in total private capital spending on infrastructure during the same period. The ratio of tax-exempt bond issuance to private- sector investment cannot, however, be directly compared with its counterpart for governmental bond financing of state and local infrastructure spending. The reason is that data on private-sector investment in infrastructure are reported within categories that may include a considerable number of capital goods that are unrelated to the accumulation of physical infrastructure and whose purchase most likely would not be eligible for tax-exempt financing. For example, the data include aircraft and equipment used in operations by privately owned airlines along with airports in the aviation category of official U.S. statistical reports for private-sector investment, but proceeds from the issuance of qualified private activity bonds cannot be used for airplanes (see 26 U.S.C. 147(e)).

Focusing solely on capital spending for structures (that is, buildings and other facilities), qualified private activity bonds issued for new investment amounted to roughly 40 percent of private capital spending on infrastructure over the 1991–2007 period. However, because that tax- exempt bond issuance exceeded investment in structures for most types of infrastructure, some of the proceeds of those bonds must have been spent on nonstructural assets, such as equipment. Thus, an estimate that would correspond to the ratio reported for state and local infrastructure spending out of tax-exempt bond proceeds would be lower (because it would reflect that additional nonstructural capital spending) and thus would be lower than the ratio for governmental bonds.[48]

Investment in electric and gas utilities, which is reported separately under the utilities category in Table 3-2, offers another example of the difficulty in matching spending by the private sector on infrastructure and the issuance of tax-exempt bonds. Almost all of that capital spending is for the generation, transmission, and distribution of electric power; however, it is unclear how closely those activities—which, in the case of electric power distribution, may be done either locally or over a multiregional electric grid—correspond to the narrow geographic restriction placed on issuance of qualified private activity bonds in that category (that is, facilities for the local furnishing of electric energy or gas whose construction can be financed with such bonds may serve at most two counties).

Table 3.2. Issuance of Qualified Private Activity Bonds for New Investment and Capital Spending by the Private Sector, Calendar Years 1991 to 2007

	Qualified Private Activity Bonds		Capital Spending by the Private Sector				Annualized Rate of Growth		
			All Infrastructure		Structures Only				
	Amount (Billions of dollars)	Share of Total Percent)	Amount (Billions of dollars)	Share ofTotal (Percent)	Amount (Billions of dollars)	Share of Total (Percent)	Qualified Private Activity Bonds (Percent)	Total Capital Spending (Percent)	Difference (Percentage points)
Health Care	199.6	53	1,190.4	44	326.3	36	5.4	6.5	-1.1
Transportation									
Aviation	58.8	16	350.5	13	31.2	3	0.7	3.9	-3.2
Docks and wharves	8.3	2	72.6	3	4.5	*	7.3	9.1	-1.9
Education	62.3	17	286.7	10	180.9	20	10.7	9.0	1.7
Environment	35.1	9	67.1	2	22.2	2	4.1	0.5	3.6
Utilities[a]									
Electric and Gas	2.3	1	724.4	27	326.6	36	-2.3	6.3	-8.6
Water, sewer, and other	5.5	1	39.7	1	26.1	3	1.8	-3.4	5.2
Total	**371.9**	**100**	**2,731.4**	**100**	**917.8**	**100**	**5.3**	**6.3**	**-1.0**

Source: Congressional Budget Office based on data from the Internal Revenue Service (for qualified private activity bonds) and the Department of Commerce (for capital spending, Bureau of Economic Analysis, Table 3.7ES and Table 3.7S, www.bea.gov/national/ FA2004/SelectTable.asp; for utilities, Census Bureau, Table 4a, www.census.gov/econ/aces/xls/2007/Full%20Report.htm).

Note: * = less than 0.5 percent.

a. Satisfactory information on investment in utilities is available only from 1994. To ensure comparability between trends in bond issuance and in capital spending by the private sector for that type of infrastructure, calculations of bond issuance and capital spending growth rates for each type of utility are limited to the 1994–2007 period.

Qualified private activity bonds have generally not become a more important means of financing private- sector investment in infrastructure. The importance of tax-exempt financing appears to have increased in particular for investment in water and sewer utilities and the environment: The annual growth rate of qualified private activity bond issuance exceeds capital spending on those types of infrastructure by 5.2 and 3.6 percentage points, respectively (see Table 3-2). However, the excess of bond issuance over spending growth disappears for that utilities category when the time period excludes 2007 (a year in which tax-exempt bonds for private investment in water utilities were issued at an exceptionally fast rate). And as with bonds issued to finance various modes of privately owned transportation—for which tax-exempt financing does not increase in importance—the issuance of environment bonds does not display a pronounced growth trend over time (see Figure 3-3 on page 21).

The use of tax-exempt bonds to finance education projects undertaken by nonprofits (that is, 501(c) (3) organizations) has increased since 1991—growth in annual bond issuance exceeds growth in capital spending by 1.7 percentage points). The same does not appear to be true for nonprofit financing of health care investment, for which annual bond sales lag capital spending by 1.1 percentage points. However, when trends in bond issuance and investment are compared from 1996—when the issuance of all types of 501(c) (3) bonds begins to grow rapidly—a somewhat clearer picture emerges. The annual growth in bond issuance exceeds capital spending by 6 percentage points for education and 1.3 percentage points for health care projects.

4. Assessing the Current Tax-Preferred Regime and an Alternative Regime

Offering a tax exemption for the interest income from bonds issued by state and local governments—governmental bonds and qualified private activity bonds—is the most well established and common way in which the federal government subsidizes borrowing by the public or private sector to invest in infrastructure. However, tax-exempt financing is not the most efficient way of delivering a subsidy: Borrowers receive only a portion of the revenues the federal government forgoes by not taxing the bonds. In addition, tax-exempt financing is regressive; the remaining portion of the forgone revenues accrues to investors in higher income tax brackets who receive greater tax savings through the exemption than would be necessary for them to purchase such bonds.

Tax-credit bonds, in contrast, do not have those disadvantages. Those bonds allow bondholders to receive a credit against federal income tax liability instead of—or in addition to—the cash interest typically paid on the bonds. Moreover, tax-credit bonds could improve the efficiency with which the federal government provides financial support to borrowers by allowing the amount of the federal subsidy to vary across projects according to the public benefits expected from them.

The amount of revenues the federal government forgoes through tax-exempt bonds is substantial. For example, the loss to the federal government from the outstanding stock of tax-exempt bonds issued to finance infrastructure is estimated to be $132 billion over the 2008–2012 period, or more than $26 billion annually. This chapter looks at how the current system of tax preferences could be made more efficient by making greater use of tax-credit bonds.

Cost Savings for States and Localities

The federal tax exemptions for interest income from governmental bonds and qualified private activity bonds enable issuers of such debt to sell bonds that pay lower rates of interest than do taxable bonds. Because purchasers of tax-exempt bonds demand a return that is no less than the after-tax yield they could obtain from comparable taxable bonds (that is, from taxable bonds of the same maturity, risk, and so on), the amount by which the return from tax-exempt bonds is lower than the yield on comparable taxable bonds depends on the income tax rate of the marginal (or market-clearing) buyer of tax- exempt bonds.[49] Box 4-1 illustrates how income tax rates affect the yields on tax-exempt bonds.

Data on tax-exempt and taxable bond transactions allow estimation of the marginal tax rate faced by the market- clearing buyer of tax-exempt bonds and, thus, the amount that states and localities save in financing costs by issuing such bonds. In 2007, the yield on (taxable) high-grade corporate bonds was 5.6 percent, and the yield on tax-exempt municipal bonds of similar creditworthiness was 4.4 percent—a difference of 1.2 percentage points, or approximately 21 percent of the taxable return.[50] The marginal tax rate at which an investor would be indifferent between purchasing a taxable bond yielding 5.6 percent and a tax-exempt bond yielding 4.4 percent is 21 percent (that is, 5.6 - (5.6 x 0.21) = 4.4); thus, one can conclude that the marginal investor pays income tax at a rate of 21 percent.[51]

In 2007, $178 billion in tax-exempt bonds was issued for new investment in infrastructure—$140 billion in governmental bonds and $38 billion in qualified private activity bonds. The difference of approximately 1.2 percentage points in the yield on tax-exempt and taxable bonds suggests that the tax exemption provided state and local governments and private-sector borrowers with a first-year interest subsidy of a bit over $2 billion on the debt they issued in 2007 to finance new infrastructure projects. Tax-exempt bonds also provide a significant subsidy to the taxpayers in higher income tax brackets who purchase them.

Revenue Loss, Inefficiency, and Regressiveness of Tax-Exempt Financing

The revenues forgone through the issuance of tax-exempt bonds are one type of implicit financial support (a tax expenditure) that the federal government provides.[52] On the basis of the outstanding stock of tax-exempt debt and an estimate of the return that would be realized if those bond holdings instead were in the form of taxable investments (usually assumed to be taxable bonds of comparable risk and maturity), tax expenditures are calculated as forgone taxable income multiplied by the average marginal income tax rate of tax-exempt bondholders.[53]

4.1. Income Tax Rates and Yields on Taxable and Tax-Exempt Bonds

The benefits from purchasing tax-exempt bonds vary among individual investors, depending on their tax bracket. If the demand for tax-exempt bonds is equal to their supply, an investor is indifferent between a tax-exempt and a taxable bond. Hence, the marginal tax rate of that market-clearing investor determines the yield on tax-exempt debt.

Consider, for example, a taxpayer with a 25 percent marginal tax rate who purchases a $1,000 taxable bond at an interest rate of 6 percent. That bond purchaser receives $60 in interest income and pays $15 in income tax, for an after-tax return of $45 and an after-tax yield of 4.5 percent. That return is the same as the net return the taxpayer would receive if he or she purchased a $1,000 tax-exempt bond paying 4.5 percent in interest. Thus, at those rates of interest, whether the bond is taxable or tax-exempt generally does not matter to that taxpayer (see the table, below).

The returns from tax-exempt debt increase with a bondholder's income tax liability. For example, a taxpayer with a 33 percent marginal tax rate who purchases a $1,000 taxable bond at an interest rate of 6 percent receives $60 in interest income and pays $20 in income tax, for a net return of $40 and an after-tax yield of 4 percent. However, that taxpayer would receive a 4.5 percent net return on a tax- exempt bond paying 4.5 percent in interest. Thus, unlike the taxpayer in the 25 percent bracket who would be indifferent between the purchase of a taxable bond paying 6 percent interest or a tax-exempt bond yielding 4.5 percent, a taxpayer in the 33 percent bracket would receive a greater benefit from that tax-exempt bond.

In contrast, a taxpayer with a 15 percent marginal tax rate would not benefit from a tax-exempt investment in this scenario, because the $45 that taxpayer would earn from a $1,000 tax-exempt bond yielding 4.5 percent would be less than the $51 he or she could obtain net of taxes by purchasing a $1,000 taxable bond yielding 6 percent (because the taxpayer would be required to pay only 15 percent—or $9— in taxes).

Rates and Yields on a $1,000 Bond

	25 Percent Marginal Tax Rate		33 Percent Marginal Tax Rate		15 Percent Marginal Tax Rate	
	Taxable	Tax-Exempt	Taxable	Tax-Exempt	Taxable	Tax-Exempt
Interest Rate	6%	4.5%	6%	4.5%	6%	4.5%
Interest Income	$60	$45	$60	$45	$60	$45
Income Tax Owed	$15	0	$20	0	$9	0
After-Tax Return	$45	$45	$40	$45	$51	$45
After-Tax Yield	4.5%	4.5%	4.0%	4.5%	5.1%	4.5%

For governmental bonds, the Joint Committee on Taxation estimates the cumulative federal tax expenditure over the 2008–2012 period to be $147 billion.[54] Bonds financing infrastructure investment (both new-money and refinancing issues combined) accounted for 64.7 percent of total governmental bond issuance from 1991 to 2007. Thus, a rough estimate of the tax expenditures over the 2008–2012 period from public infrastructure projects would be $95 billion ($147 billion multiplied by 64.7 percent), or $19 billion per year. That amount includes the approximately $1.7 billion in interest subsidy on new-money governmental bonds issued in 2007, plus the federal revenues forgone to subsidize outstanding governmental bonds that were issued in prior years (both new-money and refinancing bonds).

For qualified private activity bonds, the Joint Committee on Taxation estimates total federal tax expenditures (new-money and refunding issues combined) of $37.3 billion over the 2008–20 12 period, or almost $7.5 billion on an annual basis. That estimate is for six groups of infrastructure projects: nonprofit and qualified public education facilities ($16.0 billion); nonprofit hospital facilities ($12.1 billion); airports, docks and wharves, and mass transit facilities ($5.4 billion); sewage, water, and hazardous waste-disposal facilities ($3.1 billion); energy production facilities ($0.6 billion); and highway projects and rail-truck transfer facilities ($0.1 billion).[55]

Because there are multiple tax brackets and the market- clearing purchaser of municipal bonds will probably be in a lower bracket than most other bondholders, the loss of federal receipts is greater than the reduction in the interest costs of tax-exempt issuers. Assume, for example, that a tax-exempt bond buyer's preferred alternative investment is a taxable bond. If taxable bonds paid 6 percent in interest and the market-clearing municipal bond buyer faced a 25 percent marginal tax rate (as in the example above), the yield on a tax-exempt bond would be 4.5 percent. In that case, the revenue forgone by the federal government ($15 in lost income taxes based on a $60 interest payment taxed at 25 percent) would equal the interest savings of the tax-exempt bond issuer (who pays 4.5 percent instead of 6 percent in interest). However, some taxpayers who purchase those bonds would probably be in a higher tax bracket and consequently would produce a federal revenue loss that exceeded the savings of the bond issuer. For example, if a taxpayer in the 33 percent bracket purchased the tax-exempt bond bearing a 4.5 percent rate of interest, it would cost the federal government $20 ($60 of interest income that would have been taxed at a 33 percent rate). In that case, the $15 interest subsidy provided to the issuer of the tax-exempt bond would cost the federal government $20.[56]

Tax-exempt bonds are thus an inefficient means of providing a subsidy for debt financing from the federal point of view because a direct appropriation of funds would purchase more infrastructure on a dollar-for-dollar basis. Several analysts suggest that only about 80 percent of the tax expenditure from tax-exempt bonds actually translates into lower borrowing costs for states and localities, with the remaining 20 percent simply taking the form of a federal transfer to bondholders in higher tax brackets.[57]

If 20 percent of the federal revenue loss from tax-exempt bonds accrued to bondholders in higher tax brackets without lowering borrowing costs, and if the outstanding stock of tax-exempt debt for infrastructure during the 2008–2012 period instead took the form of tax-credit bonds designed to deliver the same amount of interest subsidy per year, the federal government would save over $26 billion (20 percent of an estimated $132 billion in tax expenditure), or more than $5 billion on an annual basis.

Using tax-exempt bonds to finance infrastructure is also regressive, because the amount by which the benefits captured by investors in either governmental or qualified private activity bonds exceeds the issuer's cost savings increases with the taxpayer's marginal tax rate. One study estimates that eliminating the tax exemption on state and local debt would reduce after-tax income primarily for taxpayers in the highest income quintile—and particularly for individuals in the top 1 percent of the income distribution.[58]

Redesigned Tax-Credit Bonds

The Congress has recently turned to tax-credit bonds as a way to finance public expenditures. Those bonds allow bondholders to receive a credit against federal income tax liability instead of—or in addition to—the cash interest typically paid on the bonds. The revenues forgone by the federal government through tax-credit bonds reduce state and local borrowing costs dollar for dollar, rather than partially accruing to investors in high marginal tax brackets (as is the case for tax-exempt debt). Thus, tax- credit bonds offer the promise of increasing the efficiency with which federal resources are allocated to support infrastructure and other investments.

Consider a Treasury-determined tax-credit bond on which the bondholder earns no interest but instead is allowed to claim a tax credit equal to 100 percent of the prevailing yield on comparable debt, which effectively subsidizes all of the issuer's interest payments. For example, the holder of a $1,000 tax-credit bond that would yield 6 percent if it was issued as taxable debt (that is, it would pay $60 in interest) would be entitled to claim a tax credit of $60. In general, a $60 tax credit would be worth $60 to a taxpayer, provided that the taxpayer had at least $60 in tax liability. However, for tax-credit bonds, the $60 credit also has to be reported as income. Reporting an additional $60 in income would cost a taxpayer in, say, the 25 percent tax bracket an additional $15 in income taxes, payable to the federal government. With the $60 tax credit that is ultimately claimed, the taxpayer nets $45 of income by holding the bond. The federal government loses $60 on the credit but recoups $15 of that amount because the $60 must be included in income, for a net cost of $45, which is exactly the net return to the taxpayer.

If the federal government had simply agreed to pay the interest on behalf of the state or local government instead of issuing a tax-credit bond, both the federal government and the bondholder/taxpayer would be in the same situation. The federal government would disburse $60 in interest payments but would recoup $15 of that in tax receipts, for a net budgetary cost of $45 as before. Similarly, the bondholder/taxpayer would receive a taxable $60 in interest and would owe $15 in taxes, for a net gain of $45 as before. The state or local government also would be in the same situation in both cases.

Because the amount of the tax credit can be set to deliver a subsidy of any value, tax-credit bonds can be structured either to provide a subsidy equivalent to that currently available from tax-exempt bonds at a lower cost (in terms of forgone federal revenue) per dollar of benefit (see Box 4-2) or, alternatively, to increase the amount of that subsidy with an unchanged revenue loss.[59] In addition, tax-credit bonds do not provide a revenue transfer to investors in high marginal tax brackets. Indeed, because the tax credit is subject to federal income tax, bondholders in higher income brackets (but above the taxpaying threshold necessary for the tax credit to be worthwhile) would, net of taxes, receive fewer credits per dollar of tax-credit bond value than would bondholders in lower income brackets (although the former group may have larger savings and investment holdings and, as a result, own more bonds).

4.2. Using Tax-Credit Bonds to Deliver an Unchanged Amount of Subsidy at Lower Cost to the Federal Government

Tax-credit bonds can be structured to deliver any amount of federal subsidy and, in theory, could provide the same amount of federal subsidy to issuers that tax-exempt bonds are estimated to provide—and with a lower revenue loss. (Important constraints to setting such a credit rate in practice are discussed below.) The return provided by a tax-credit bond has two taxable components: an interest payment from the borrower and a tax credit from the federal government. To maintain the federal subsidy currently available to borrowers through tax-exempt debt, the tax- credit bond would have to meet two conditions:

- The interest payment due from borrowers would have to be the same as it would have been if the bonds had been issued as tax-exempt debt; and
- The value to bond buyers of the sum of that interest payment and the tax credit would have to equal the interest income on a comparable taxable bond.

To meet those conditions, the tax-credit rate would be expressed as a percentage of the borrower's interest cost, $t/(1-t)$, where t is the marginal income tax bracket of the market-clearing bondholder. In 2007, for example, t was 21 percent. (The yield on high- grade taxable corporate bonds was 5.6 percent, and the yield on tax-exempt municipal bonds of similar creditworthiness was 4.4 percent—a difference of approximately 1.2 percentage points, or 21 percent of the taxable return.) With an implied marginal tax rate of 21 percent for the market-clearing tax-exempt bondholder, the tax-credit rate would be 26.5 percent (0.21/1-0.21).

Given a taxable rate of interest on a comparable bond of 5.6 percent, all purchasers of a $1,000 tax-credit bond would receive a taxable interest payment of $44 from the borrower—the same 4.4 percent in interest that the borrower would have paid on a tax-exempt bond for which the implied market-clearing marginal tax rate was 21 percent—and a tax credit of $11.66 (which equals the credit rate of 26.5 percent multiplied by 4.4 percent multiplied by $1,000).

The federal government would not lose any revenues other than the amount of the credit, because both the borrower's interest payment of $44 and the tax credit of $11.66 would be taxed at each bondholder's marginal tax rate—as would be the $55.66 of interest income on an equivalent taxable bond. The interest payment and tax credit received by the market-clearing bond buyer in this example would be taxed at the rate of 21 percent, and the bond buyer would receive $44 after taxes (that is, $34.80 + $9.20). The $11.66 tax credit would substitute for the $11.66 of interest costs that the borrower would have had to pay on a taxable bond; it would also equal the savings that the borrower would have realized by issuing a tax-exempt bond. The federal government's cost would equal the tax credit—that is, the interest savings—regardless of whether the marginal tax rate of the bond purchaser was 21 percent or a higher rate.

The tax-credit bonds in this example are assumed to replace tax-exempt debt in its entirety. If that is not the case and both tax-credit and tax-exempt bonds are issued contemporaneously, then bond buyers with high marginal income tax liability would have an incentive to continue to purchase tax-exempt debt because, as long as the market-clearing buyer was in a lower tax bracket, those bonds would be more desirable to them. As a result, tax-credit and tax-exempt bonds would not be directly interchangeable in many investors' portfolios, and it would be necessary to determine the yield that would clear the market for tax-credit and tax-exempt bonds individually in order to estimate the potential gains (from lowering the federal government's revenue loss) through the newly designed tax-credit bonds. An additional factor in the analysis is a potential change in the pool of potential tax-preferred bond buyers, which could occur if the tax credits in question could be stripped and sold or if the tax-credit bonds were taxable direct-pay issues. In either case, the number of prospective buyers of tax- credit bonds could increase to include entities such as tax-exempt organizations and foreign persons, who previously would have had no incentive to invest in tax-exempt debt.

For additional information on this topic, see Congressional Budget Office, *Tax-Credit Bonds and the Federal Cost of Financing Public Expenditures* (July 2004), p. 6; and Joint Committee on Taxation, *Present Law and Issues Related to Infrastructure Finance,* JCX-83-08 (October 24, 2008), pp. 32–34, www.jct.gov/x-83-08.pdf.

Beyond making federal tax preferences for borrowing more cost-effective, tax-credit bonds can increase the efficiency with which the federal government supports debt financing of state and local investment in infrastructure in another way as well. Tax-credit bonds have traditionally provided a large subsidy to issuers, approaching 100 percent of interest costs for most types of tax-credit bonds—and a much larger subsidy than is available through issuing tax-exempt debt.[60] The amount of the subsidy provided by a tax-credit bond, however, can be varied across different types of projects by setting the level of the credit in accordance with the public benefits expected from each. The substantial differences among infrastructure facilities and the services they provide— even within groups of publicly or privately owned infrastructure—suggest that those efficiency gains could be sizable.

For example, local governments' investment in local mass transit systems benefits from the same federal tax-exempt financing as does their capital spending on the interstate highway system, even though public benefits provided at the national level are probably quite different between the two types of infrastructure. A similar reasoning applies to private-sector investments eligible for tax preferences. Although current law does not impose a "public purpose" requirement on qualified private activity bonds, many of the original facilities eligible for tax-exempt financing under the Internal Revenue Code of 1986 (for example, airports, docks and wharves, and solid waste facilities) provide services that probably include some public benefits. However, because the private-sector owners of even within groups of publicly or privately owned infrastructure—suggest that those efficiency gains could be sizable.

For example, local governments' investment in local mass transit systems benefits from the same federal tax-exempt financing as does their capital spending on the interstate highway system, even though public benefits provided at the national level are probably quite different between the two types of infrastructure. A similar reasoning applies to private-sector investments eligible for tax preferences. Although current law does not impose a "public purpose" requirement on qualified private activity bonds, many of the original facilities eligible for tax-exempt financing under the Internal Revenue Code of 1986 (for example, airports, docks and wharves, and solid waste facilities) provide services that probably include some public benefits. However, because the private-sector owners of that infrastructure can capture through user fees and other charges a sizable portion of the value of the services they provide, the public benefits from those investments may be small relative to infrastructure provided by government, and only a small subsidy—if any—may be efficient.[61]

In addition, over the past several decades the Congress has expanded the list of private-sector activities eligible for federal tax preferences and, as a result, 26 categories of private activities are now eligible for a tax preference on borrowing (that figure includes the preferential rules for certain geographic areas such as enterprise zones, the New York Liberty Zone, the Gulf Opportunity Zone, and qualified forestry conservation areas). As tax-preferred financing is extended to private activities that are more narrowly defined, the amount of public benefits from them is likely to decline and so too the economically efficient amount of federal subsidy. Consequently, allowing the subsidy rate to vary by type of infrastructure financed and the public returns expected from it could increase the efficiency of tax-preferred financing of infrastructure projects undertaken by either the public or the private sector.

End Notes

[1] The excess of tax-exempt yields over taxable Treasury yields in 2008 reflected an extreme "flight to quality" that has rarely been seen in U.S. debt markets. Uncertainty in the markets caused investors to move away from investments they believed to be riskier, including tax-exempt municipal bonds, and into those perceived as safer—Treasury securities in particular. As a result, yields on some Treasury bonds fell to levels below yields on tax-exempt municipal bonds that have the same maturity.

[2] As the issuers of tax-exempt debt expand the pool of bond purchasers until it is sufficiently large to exhaust the amount of debt they are bringing to market, they draw in bond buyers from ever- lower income tax brackets by raising the interest rate enough so that the yield on tax-exempt bonds is competitive with the after- tax rate of return on taxable instruments for investors in those lower brackets. As a result, the marginal buyer of tax-exempt bonds will typically demand a tax-exempt yield that exceeds what an individual in a higher income tax bracket requires to purchase those bonds.

[3] For a broader discussion of infrastructure, see Congressional Budget Office, *Issues and Options in Infrastructure Investment* (May 2008), pp. 2–4. Three types of infrastructure examined in that paper—telecommunications, postal facilities, and prisons—are not included here because available data are not sufficiently detailed to allow analysis of the tax-exempt debt issued for them (in the case of prisons) or because they are almost entirely provided by the federal government (postal facilities) or the private sector (telecommunications) and a tax preference for the debt incurred through that capital spending does not exist.

[4] For other data on investment by the federal government, which may include spending on facilities and equipment in addition to the spending reported in this study, see *Budget of the United States Government, Fiscal Year 2009: Analytical Perspectives*, pp. 57–68, and *Historical Tables*, Tables 9-1 to 9-6.

[5] Public benefits stand in contrast to private benefits, which can be assessed and charged to the individuals receiving them and for which those individuals are willing to pay. Other terms for public benefits are "social benefits," "collective consumption benefits," and "positive spillover effects."

[6] See Congressional Budget Office, *Issues and Options in Infrastructure Investment*, Figure 1, p. 6.

[7] In contrast, the federal government is a more important source than states and localities for investment in environmental infrastructure, such as water and other natural resources (for example, dams).

[8] More precisely, because the federal government allows each state to issue up to a specified amount of tax-preferred debt each year for certain investments by the private sector, states and localities generally select the particular projects within their jurisdiction that will receive that financing. See Chapter 2 for further discussion of restrictions on private-sector issuance of tax-preferred bonds.

[9] For the most recent estimates of federal tax expenditures from tax preferences on municipal bonds and from other provisions of the tax code, see Joint Committee on Taxation, *Estimates of Federal Tax Expenditures for Fiscal Years 2008–2012*, JCS-2-08 (October 31, 2008), pp. 48–72, www.house.gov/jct/s-2-08.pdf; and *Budget of the United States Government, Fiscal Year 2010: Analytical Perspectives*, Table 19-2, pp. 303–306. Although they apply slightly different methodologies, the two sets of estimates are usually very close in value.

[10] For the most recent data on the distribution of federal grants and loan subsidies across states, see *Budget of the United States Government, Fiscal Year 2009: Analytical Perspectives*, Tables 8-2 to 8-36, pp. 126–156.

[11] However, the federal government does place limits on the annual amount of some tax-exempt bonds that states and localities may issue to finance investment by the private sector.

[12] A recent modification to the tax-preferred bond regime is the direct-pay feature of certain new bonds authorized by the American Recovery and Reinvestment Act of 2009 (Public Law 111-5), under which the government makes direct payments to bond issuers (see Chapter 2).

[13] An estimate of the amount of output forgone by making interest income tax-exempt—and the corresponding economic or social return beyond that obtained by private investors in order to make the tax preference generate a net public benefit—can be obtained by considering how much higher the gross return to the capital invested in a project would have to be in order to warrant that investment in the absence of the tax exemption. For an example of such calculations, see Dennis Zimmerman, *The Private Use of Tax-Exempt Bonds: Controlling Public Subsidy of Private Activity* (Washington, D.C.: Urban Institute Press, 1991), pp. 124–128.

[14] Indian tribal governments also can issue tax-exempt bonds to finance "essential governmental functions," and the American Recovery and Reinvestment Act of 2009 contains a provision that permits them to issue **tribal economic development bonds** for any purpose for which a state or local government can issue tax- exempt bonds. The cumulative amount of tribal economic development bonds issued nationwide may not exceed $2 billion.

[15] See Commissioner v. Shamberg's Estate, 144 F.2d 998 (2d Cir. 1944), cert. denied, 323 U.S. 792 (1945). A qualified governmental unit may also establish an entity with limited sovereign powers (for example, an economic development authority) to issue bonds on its behalf. Such "on behalf of" corporations developed historically because some state laws and constitutions defined the purposes for which the state could issue bonds more narrowly than federal tax law did. For example, a specially constituted nonprofit corporation acting on behalf of a qualified governmental unit might own, operate, and issue tax-exempt debt to finance a local airport. The general requirements that those nonprofit corporations must satisfy are specified in two administrative determinations of the Internal Revenue Service (see Rev. Rul. 63-20, 1963-1 C.B. 24; Rev. Proc. 82-26, 1982-1 C.B. 476).

[16] In contrast to governmental bonds, qualified private activity bonds do not benefit from a full tax exemption because the interest income from them (other than qualified 501(c) (3) bonds issued after August 7, 1986), is a preference item for purposes of calculating the alternative minimum tax (AMT). However, as a result of a change made by the American Recovery and Reinvestment Act of 2009, interest on private activity bonds (other than certain refunding bonds) issued after December 31, 2008, and before January 1, 2011, is not treated as an AMT preference item; see sec. 57(a)(5)(C)(vi). All section references are to the Internal Revenue Code of 1986 (the Code) unless otherwise indicated.

[17] In addition to financing infrastructure projects that fall under the definition of this analysis, states and localities also issue tax- exempt debt for public housing and other, more general purposes.

[18] Sec. 141(a).

[19] Local governments may structure the financing of some projects—notably sports stadiums—so that the bonds financing them fail the private business test. Governments can do that by making the private business or sports team using the stadium responsible for only a very small share (less than 10 percent) of the repayment of the loan *or* by supporting the debt service on the bonds with generally applicable taxes. The Joint Committee on Taxation has identified elimination of the private payment prong of the private business test as a way of preventing that practice. See Joint Committee on Taxation, *Options to Improve Tax Compliance and Reform Tax Expenditures*, JCS-02-05 (January 27, 2005), pp. 353–358.

[20] Private loans include both business and other (for example, personal) uses and payments by private persons; however, in the case of business uses and payments, all private loans also constitute private business uses and payments subject to the private business test.

[21] For a discussion of the law and economics of tax-exempt private activity bonds, see Dennis Zimmerman, *The Private Use of Tax-Exempt Bonds: Controlling Public Subsidy of Private Activity* (Washington, D.C.: Urban Institute Press, 1991).

[22] Rules for the issuance of tax-exempt bonds by 501(c) (3) organizations are found in sec. 145 of the Code.

[23] A state-level volume cap is allocated statutorily among "issuing authorities," which can be state agencies or other qualified governmental units. The annual issuance level for local governments, for example, is based on their population, although the state governor or legislature can reallocate issuance among them. For further details, see sec. 146.

[24] See sec. 146(d)(1); Rev. Proc. 2008-66, 2008-45 I.R.B.

[25] For more discussion of these and other limitations on the issuance of qualified private activity bonds, see Joint Committee on Taxation, *Present Law and Issues Related to Infrastructure Finance,* JCX-83-08 (October 24, 2008), www.house.gov/jct/ x-83-08.pdf, and *Present Law and Background Relating to State and Local Government Bonds,* JCX-14-06 (March 16, 2006), www.jct.gov/publications.html?func=startdown&id

[26] Under special rules, the refunding of bonds issued before August 8, 1986, and the refunding of certain bonds issued before September 1, 1986, are not subject to the alternative minimum tax.

[27] Midwest Tax-Credit Bonds were authorized by the Heartland Disaster Relief Act of 2008, Div. C., Title VII, Subtitle A. of Pub. Law 110-343, 122 Stat. 3912. They may be issued in 2009 by any state (or any agency or other entity acting on behalf of a state) in which a Midwestern disaster area is located and may be issued to make payments of principal or interest on outstanding state debt.

[28] Authority to issue Clean Renewable Energy Bonds under sec. 54 sunsets on December 31, 2009.

[29] For a more detailed discussion of the law relating to certain tax- credit bonds, see Joint Committee on Taxation, *Present Law and Issues Related to Infrastructure Finance,* pp. 18–22. That discussion predates the American Recovery and Reinvestment Act of 2009, however; for an explanation of the provisions of that act, see House of Representatives, *Making Supplemental Appropriations for Job Preservation and Creation, Infrastructure Investment, Energy Efficiency and Science, Assistance to the Unemployed, and State and Local Fiscal Stabilization, for the Fiscal Year Ending September 30, 2009, and for Other Purposes,* H.R. Conf. Rep. No. 111-16 to accompany H.R. 1 (February 12, 2009).

[30] See, generally, IRS Notice 2009-15, 2009-6 I.R.B. "The Treasury Department will determine and announce credit rates for tax- credit bonds daily for purposes of §§ 54, 54A, 1400N(l), and other similar provisions, based on its estimate of the yields on outstanding bonds from market sectors selected by the Treasury Department in its discretion that have an investment grade rating of between A and BBB for bonds of a similar maturity for the business day immediately preceding the sale date of the tax-credit bonds."

[31] Qualified tax-credit bonds are Qualified Zone Academy Bonds, New CREBs, QECs, Qualified Forestry Conservation Bonds, and Qualified School Construction Bonds. See sec. 54A(d)(1).

[32] Original issue discount is the excess of an obligation's stated redemption price at maturity over the obligation's issue price (sec. 1273(a)).

[33] The American Recovery and Reinvestment Act also created another type of qualified Build America Bond—Recovery Zone Economic Development Bonds, which have a credit rate of 45 percent rather than 35 percent (sec. 1400U-2). Again, because the issuer does not pay tax, the issuer's net interest cost for one of those bonds with a face value of $1,000 and a coupon of $60 would be $33 (compared with $39 in the case of other qualified Build America Bonds and $44.40 in the case of Build America Bonds that are not qualified bonds).

[34] Statistics on tax-exempt bonds are available at www.irs.gov/ taxexemptbond/index.html. The data on bond issuance used in this study reflect debt of long-term maturity (13 months or more); that type of debt is generally used to finance construction or other capital improvement projects and is reported to the IRS by tax- exempt bond issuers on Form 8038-G (Information Return for Tax-Exempt Governmental Obligations) and Form 8038 (Infor-

mation Return for Tax-Exempt Private Activity Bond Issues). Information on tax-credit bonds is reported to the IRS by individuals and businesses claiming those tax credits on Form 8912 (Credit to Holders of Tax Credit Bonds) and, for holders of Qualified Zone Academy Bonds claiming that credit before the 2008 tax year, on Form 8860 (Qualified Zone Academy Bond Credit).

[35] The issuance of some qualified private activity bonds reported in separate categories on IRS Form 8038 has been combined in this study to facilitate comparison with the corresponding data reported for governmental bonds; details are provided in Box 3-2 on page 23. Information on the purposes of such bonds is probably more specific because qualified private activity bonds are subject to more restrictions than are governmental bonds (such as volume caps), and those restrictions are often dependent on the particular type of project being financed.

[36] Data from the IRS show that debt-financing costs for governmental bonds average about 2 percent of the value of the bonds issued; see, for example, Table 3, www.irs.gov/pub/irs-soi/07bd03gb.xls. For qualified private activity bonds, such use of the proceeds is capped at 2 percent by law.

[37] From 1991 to 2007, tax-exempt bonds issued for refunding existing infrastructure debt amounted to $932 billion for governmental bonds and $225 billion for qualified private activity bonds. Beneficiaries of those bond proceeds may have applied some of the cost savings from that refunding to make additional investment in infrastructure. However, unless that investment drew upon a tax-exempt bond sale (with the savings in interest costs from the refinancing applied to service the new debt), the contribution of refunding bonds to capital spending on infrastructure would not be reflected in this analysis.

[38] Although water supply and sewer systems might both be considered utility services, the IRS puts the proceeds of governmental bonds issued for sewer projects in the "environment" category. That classification is maintained when this study reports the issuance of state and local bonds and capital spending by type of infrastructure (see Table 3-1 on page 25). In reporting the proceeds of qualified private activity bonds issued for utilities and environmental projects, however, this study classifies sewer systems as a utility because that is how the Census Bureau and the Bureau of Economic Analysis report data on private-sector investment in infrastructure (see Figure 3-3 on page 21, Box 3-2 on page 23, and Table 3-2 on page 27).

[39] According to an unpublished IRS analysis, education and health care projects accounted for approximately 28 percent and 17 percent, respectively, of the total new-money issuance of nonhospital 501(c) (3) bonds over the 1996–2006 period. A study by the Government Accountability Office (GAO) found a very different allocation: 15.5 percent of nonhospital 501(c) (3) bonds issued in 2003 and 2004 went to education and 37.2 percent went to health care. See Government Accountability Office, *Tax-Exempt Status of Certain Bonds Merits Reconsideration, and Apparent Noncompliance with Issuance Cost Limitations Should Be Addressed,* GAO-08-364 (February 2008). The IRS and GAO analyses covered different time periods; in addition, their results may differ because of how each study allocated the proceeds of nonhospital 501(c)(3) bonds. The IRS analysis determined the use of bond proceeds on the basis of the "primary tax-exempt purpose" of nonprofit organizations benefiting from them (as reported on IRS Form 990); the GAO study used information on the industry classification of the "projects financed" by the bond proceeds (reported on IRS Form 8038). The IRS's method is consistent with how the data on private-sector investment collected by the Bureau of Economic Analysis and used in this study are classified by type of infrastructure.

[40] See Congressional Budget Office, "Nonprofit Hospitals and Tax Arbitrage," letter to the Honorable William "Bill" M. Thomas (December 6, 2006). The exclusion from income for interest on state and local bonds does not apply to any arbitrage bond (sec. 103(a) and (b)(2)). An arbitrage bond is defined as any bond that is part of an issue if any proceeds of the issue are reasonably expected to be used (or intentionally are used) to acquire higher

yielding investments or to replace funds that are used to acquire higher yielding investments. In general, arbitrage profits may be earned only during specified periods (for example, defined "temporary periods") before funds are needed for the purpose of the borrowing or on specified types of investments (for example, "reasonably required reserve or replacement funds"). Subject to limited exceptions, investment profits that are earned during those periods or on such investments must be rebated to the federal government. However, tax-exempt bond issuers can engage in a less direct form of tax arbitrage when they finance their activities by issuing tax-exempt debt rather than selling off assets that generate returns at taxable rates.

41 See Thornton Matheson, "Qualified Zone Academy Bond Tax Credit Usage in 2005," *Statistics of Income Bulletin* (Spring 2009), pp. 106–109. QZAB proceeds can finance projects undertaken at a "qualified zone academy," which is basically a publicly run school in an economically disadvantaged neighborhood that has the support (both in designing the curriculum and providing equipment) of private business. Those projects can include activities related to infrastructure investment—such as rehabilitation and repair of the facility—and also spending to develop course materials and train teachers.

42 See Peter Schroeder, "Not-So-Warm Embrace," *The Bond Buyer* (March 30, 2009), www.bondbuyer.com/ article.html?id=20090327 1L87BV5E.

43 Tax-exempt bonds that rely on tax receipts for their repayment are known as **general obligation bonds.** However, not all tax-exempt bonds are general obligation bonds, because some types of infrastructure lend themselves to repayment through user fees better than do others and are thus less reliant on taxes for their funding. For example, repayment of the infrastructure debt financed by qualified private activity bonds—nonprofit schools and hospitals, utilities, and certain modes of transportation (such as airports)—is done through the user fees and other charges collected by the private entity responsible for the facility. In such cases, the bonds are known as **revenue bonds.** Governments with the power to tax may also issue revenue rather than general obligation bonds, but they restrict the debt-service funds to only those funds from the governmental entity that generates the revenues. In contrast to general obligation bonds, in such cases the government itself does not pledge its own credit to pay the debt.

44 For that assumption to allow for an accurate inference about the importance of tax-exempt bond financing to infrastructure investment, the rate at which the proceeds of bonds issued before 1991 are spent over the 199 1–2007 period must match the spending rate after 2007 for the proceeds of bonds issued during that period.

45 The use of tax-exempt bonds to finance local investment in water supply and sewage systems (classified in the "utilities" and "environment" categories of governmental bond issuance, respectively) seems to be very common (as is the use of state revolving funds). For example, according to a January 10, 2005, survey of U.S. cities with a mayoral form of government and a population of 30,000 or more, cities that had made a major capital investment in a water supply or a wastewater treatment system during the five years before the survey financed that spending with either general obligation bonds (for 25.8 percent of projects) or revenue bonds (for 41.3 percent of projects); for investments planned in the next five years, the corresponding percentages were 24.9 percent and 44.7 percent. (Because those bonds may be used in tandem and with other funding sources, such as charges to current users and general tax receipts, the shares cannot be added to obtain the overall contribution of tax-exempt financing to that capital spending.) In contrast, for only about 1 percent of cases of past and future investment were tax-exempt or taxable private activity bonds reported to be a source of financing. See United States Conference of Mayors' Urban Water Council, *National City Water Survey 2005* (Washington, D.C.: United States Conference of Mayors, November 15, 2005), pp. 18–19, www.usmayors.org/ 74thWinterMeeting/NationalCityWaterSurvey2005.pdf.

46 Approximately three-quarters of state and local capital spending on highways originates with the states. See Government Accountability Office, *Trends in Federal and State Capital*

Investment in Highways, GAO-03-744R (June 18, 2003), pp. 3–10. The data on state highway spending and revenues come from the Federal Highway Administration, Highways Statistics Series, www.fhwa.dot.gov/policy/ohpi/qffinance.cfm. For data on bond issuance, see Section IY: Finance, Table SF-1, various years, www.fhwa.dot.gov/policy/ohpi/hss/hsspubs.cfm. In 2006, states issued $11.9 billion of bonds for new highway investment, compared with $5.6 billion issued by localities in 2005 (both numbers are in current dollars; data on bonds issued by localities are reported every other year).

[47] Over the 2001–2006 period, states' issuance of highway construction bonds (in constant dollars) fell by about 1.7 percentage points on an annualized basis, which is close to the decline of 1.5 percentage points in inflation-adjusted state and local highway spending.

[48] Qualified private activity bonds may still be very important for financing some types of capital spending on infrastructure. For example, studies suggest that tax-exempt bond proceeds going to private investment in airports over the past decade may have been of comparable importance to other types of funding for that purpose, such as federal grants or airport user charges. See ACI-NA Policy Center, *Reforming the Federal Tax Treatment of Airport Bonds: Executive Summary* (February 28, 2006), available on request from the Airports Council International—North America, www.aci-na.org. Note, however, that the various sources of funding may not be entirely independent, because airport user charges can be used to secure or pay off loans. In addition, federal grants through the Airport Improvement Program are more important to smaller airports than to larger ones, because the latter are better able to tap financial markets to fund their capital projects. See Robert S. Kirk, *Airport Improvement Program: Issues for Congress,* CRS Report for Congress RL33891 (Congressional Research Service, February 26, 2007), p. 7.

[49] Bond issuers must pay the market-clearing bond buyer an interest rate that matches the supply of tax-exempt bonds with the demand for them; that interest rate is therefore the yield that all issuers of comparable tax-exempt debt must pay.

[50] See Joint Committee on Taxation, *Present Law and Issues Related to Infrastructure Finance*, JCX-83-08 (October 24, 2008), p. 28, www.house.gov/jct/x-83-08.pdf. See also *Economic Report of the President* (transmitted to the Congress in January 2008), Table B-73, p. 312.

[51] The precision of the estimated tax rate depends heavily on the comparability of the yields on tax-exempt and taxable bonds. For example, because the data on both tax-exempt and taxable interest rates used in this analysis are averages across bonds in each category that may still vary somewhat because of risk, time to maturity, fixed versus variable interest payments, and other bond-specific factors, the marginal tax rate they imply for the market-clearing buyer of tax-exempt bonds may not be equal to a rate specified by the tax code. However, several potential sources of bias probably offset each other to a large degree—at least in the calculations in this analysis. For example, if the yield on tax-exempt bonds included a premium relative to the yield on taxable corporate debt because municipal bonds are less liquid—which can happen if state and local borrowers are more heterogeneous and issue debt in smaller amounts than corporations do—that would bias downward the estimated tax rate of the market-clearing buyer of tax-exempt bonds. The reason is that the inflated yield on a tax-exempt bond that included such a liquidity premium relative to more liquid taxable debt would result in a smaller observed spread between the returns of taxable and tax-exempt bonds and consequently would understate the pure tax benefit necessary to make a tax-exempt purchase advantageous. Potentially working in the opposite direction—that is, inflating the estimated tax rate of the marketclearing buyer of tax-exempt bonds—would be a greater creditworthiness of municipalities relative to that of issuers of taxable corporate bonds, even though each type of bond received the same rating for credit risk (see Moody's Investors Service, *Moody's US Municipal Bond Rating Scale,* November 2002). Comparing two such bonds would produce too large an observed spread between taxable and tax-exempt bond returns, because the yield on taxable bonds would include a risk premium that the tax-exempt bond did not.

[52] States also typically exempt from taxation the interest income from municipal bonds issued in-state and, in a few cases, those issued out-of-state as well. However, income tax rates are much lower at the state level than at the federal level and, hence, so too would be any revenues forgone by the state government through such exemptions. For data on tax rates and tax exemptions offered by individual states, see Thomson Financial, *The Bond Buyer Yearbook* (New York: SourceMedia, various years).

[53] Such calculations do not incorporate the behavioral responses of bondholders to a removal of the tax exemption on interest income, and they are subject to other assumptions. See Leonard E. Burman, "Is the Tax Expenditure Concept Still Relevant?" *National Tax Journal*, vol. 56, no. 3 (September 2003), pp. 613–627.

[54] See Joint Committee on Taxation, *Estimates of Federal Tax Expenditures for Fiscal Years 2008–2012*, JCS-2-08 (October 31, 2008), www.house.gov/jct/s-2-08.pdf.

[55] Ibid.

[56] The yield on taxable bonds is typically used as a proxy for the return from a taxable investment that tax-exempt bondholders would make if that exemption was removed. Some analysts suggest that using a different alternative taxable investment could result in a smaller estimate of tax expenditures. See, for example, James Poterba and Arturo Ramirez Verdugo, *Portfolio Substitution and the Revenue Cost of Exempting State and Local Government Interest Payments from Federal Income Tax*, Working Paper 14439 (Cambridge, Mass.: National Bureau of Economic Research, October 2008), www.nber.org/papers/w14439. However, if tax-exempt bondholders face different marginal income tax rates, then such findings still do not alter the conclusion that the federal government loses more in revenue from the issuance of tax-exempt bonds than state and local governments gain. For example, Poterba and Ramirez Verdugo estimate that 53 percent of the outstanding stock of tax-exempt bonds in 2003 was held by households with marginal tax rates in excess of 30 percent and that the holdings of the remaining tax-exempt bonds were distributed throughout most of the lower income tax brackets (see Table 6 on p. 31 of their paper). More recently, on the basis of tax-exempt interest income reported by taxpayers to the IRS, the staff of the Joint Committee on Taxation projects that approximately 4.9 million individual taxpayers will report about $71 billion in tax-exempt interest for 2009. Of those totals, 3.2 million taxpayers are projected to be in marginal tax brackets of 25 percent or higher in 2009 and will report in excess of $56 billion in tax-exempt interest. Joint Committee on Taxation, *Present Law and Issues Related to Infrastructure Finance*, footnote 40, p. 27.

[57] See Dennis Zimmerman, *The Private Use of Tax-Exempt Bonds: Controlling Public Subsidy of Private Activity* (Washington, D.C.: Urban Institute Press, 1991), pp. 103–104; and Poterba and Ramirez Verdugo, *Portfolio Substitution and the Revenue Cost of Exempting State and Local Government Interest Payments from Federal Income Tax*. The latter authors estimate that in 2003 the marginal income tax rate of the average tax-exempt bondholder was 26.8 percent and the tax rate faced by the market-clearing municipal bond buyer was between 13 percent and 22 percent (see pp. 3 and 16 in Poterba and Ramirez Verdugo). Their analysis is restricted to households and does not include corporations, which account for between one-quarter and one-third of the total tax expenditure from tax-exempt bonds estimated for the 2008–2012 period.

[58] The decrease in after-tax income that results from eliminating the tax exemption is estimated to be at or near zero for all but the top income quintile, where after-tax income falls by 0.24 percent for that quintile and 0.50 percent for the top 1 percent. See Leonard Burman, Eric Toder, and Christopher Geissler, *How Big Are Total Individual Income Tax Expenditures, and Who Benefits from Them?* Discussion Paper No. 31 (Washington, D.C.: Urban Institute, December 2008), p. 11, www.urban.org/publications/ 1001234.html.

[59] The taxable Build America Bonds authorized by the American Recovery and Reinvestment Act of 2009, which are to be issued by state and local governments in 2009 and 2010 and which provide a 35 percent tax credit to either purchasers or issuers (in the latter case, if all

of the proceeds are used to finance capital expenditures and the issuer elects to receive the credit) illustrate to some degree how more of the federal tax expenditure from tax preferences on governmental bonds can be provided to borrowers. In addition, the direct-pay feature of certain Build America Bonds, under which the government makes direct payments to bond issuers rather than providing a tax credit to bondholders, allows the amount of subsidy provided by the tax preference to show up as an outlay in the federal budget. However, because the credit amount on those bonds is almost certainly higher than the marginal income tax rate of the average tax-exempt bondholder, the federal subsidy is larger.

[60] For example, Qualified Zone Academy Bonds provided borrowers with an annual subsidy equal to roughly 6 to 7 percentage points of bond yield between 1998 and 2005; in contrast, the annual interest subsidy from tax-exempt bonds during that time ranged from 1 percent to 2 percent. See Thornton Matheson, "Qualified Zone Academy Bond Tax Credit Usage in 2005," *Statistics of Income Bulletin* (Spring 2009), Figure D, p. 109; and Joint Committee on Taxation, *Present Law and Issues Related to Infrastructure Finance*, p. 28.

[61] The cost of financing investment with tax-preferred bonds is similar for public and private projects: Yields on qualified private activity bonds exceed those of comparable governmental bonds by 5 to 20 basis points, depending on the maturity of the bond (see Poterba and Ramirez Verdugo, *Portfolio Substitution and the Revenue Cost of Exempting State and Local Government Interest Payments from Federal Income Tax*, p. 5). The Congress does set some limits on the federal financing subsidy provided to many types of private-sector investments; among other restrictions, it places a cap on the dollar amount of bonds that can be issued annually. However, qualified private activity bonds for many types of private-sector infrastructure projects (including airports; docks and wharves; and activities related to education, hospitals, and health care undertaken by qualified 501(c) (3) organizations) are not subject to the volume cap.

Chapter Sources

The following chapters have been previously published:

Chapter 1 – This is an edited, excerpted and augmented edition of a United States Joint Committee on Taxation document, (JCX- 14-06), for the hearing before the Subcommittee on Select Revenue Measures of the House Committee on Ways and Means, dated March 16, 2006.

Chapter 2 – This is an edited, excerpted and augmented edition of a United States Joint Committee on Taxation document, (JCX- 83-08), for the hearing before the House Committee on Ways and Means, dated October 29, 2008.

Chapter 3 – This is an edited, excerpted and augmented edition of a Joint United States Congressional Budget Office/Joint Committee on Taxation Study, Pub. No. 4005, dated October 2008.

INDEX

C

D

G

H

I

J

K

L

M

N

O

P

Q

R

S

Y